Adventures in Retirement

A hilarious journey into the unknown world of excess time, limited responsibilities and an uncertain future.

by Lawrence G. Doyle

LGDoyle.com

Copyright © 2017 Lawrence Doyle.

All rights reserved.

No part of this publication may be reproduced, stored, or copied
without written permission from the author, except by a reviewer
who wishes to quote a brief passage in connection with a review. The
names of people appearing in the book have been changed.

170822

Table of Contents

Exit strategies

I've always dreamed of a retirement funded in part by a really large, golden parachute-style buyout— something so big it would not only guarantee financial security but also would pay for all the wonderful things I hope to do with the rest of my life.

Most people think of the buyout option as being reserved solely for CEOs who negotiate cushy exit deals before even accepting a job, or for the lucky few offered early retirement incentives in tough times. But there is a third option, so rare it's rarely discussed. It involves being just crazy enough that the employer really wants you to leave but just sane enough that they can't find grounds for firing you. This is a *very* fine line to walk, but it can be done. I know. I've witnessed it.

Many years ago, I worked with a woman I'll call Susan. She was in her mid-50s and had been with the organization for many years. Everyone liked her. She tackled every project with enthusiasm and never failed to greet each co-worker with a warm "hello."

Unbeknownst to us, however, Susan was also a little crazy or very clever or possibly both. At some point, she started coming in early, well before the rest of us. Her morning routine began with her going to the kitchen and boiling a small pot of water. She would carry the steaming pot back to her cubicle, crawl under her desk and then carefully pour the boiling liquid onto the carpet. She did this every morning for weeks, possibly months. Then one day, someone of some importance happened to walk by her desk and found himself sloshing through the carpet swamp that had formed around her cubicle.

Building maintenance was alerted. They thoroughly studied the problem but could find no immediate cause. Water was obviously coming from somewhere but the puddle was in a part of the building where there were no water pipes. Even more perplexing was the discovery that the carpet swamp seemed to grow larger with each passing day. A staff team was assembled. Meetings were held. Samples were taken. The exterior of the building was checked for holes; the interior for leaks. Theories were offered. Each was disproved. Finally, they asked Susan if she had any idea how the carpet got so wet. She explained to them in a matter-of-fact way that every morning she poured boiling water on it.

When asked why, Susan explained it was to "kill the bugs."

"What bugs?" they asked.

"The ones that live under my desk," she replied.

A new staff team was pulled together. Meetings were held. Emails were circulated. An action plan was developed. An exterminator was called in. Samples were taken. Tests were run. The result? No bugs could be found.

The team happily reported these findings to Susan.

She seemed amused by this, "Of course you didn't see any bugs, they're invisible!"

Ours was a compassionate office. Instead of termination, senior management exacted a promise from her that she would stop pouring water on the carpets and would seek mental health counseling. She complied. Management breathed a sigh of relief—too soon, as it turned out.

Susan's counselor encouraged her to express her feelings through poetry. This she did, taking it a step further by posting her poems on the outer wall of her cubicle. These were cleverly written sonnets that expressed the full range of her inner demons and which could easily, but not definitively, have been interpreted as vague threats directed toward two people highly placed in the organization.

Management faced a choice. They could pursue a complicated legal effort to fire an employee seeking mental health services or they could make her an offer to leave that she couldn't refuse. They chose the latter.

Before Susan could even begin to pack her personal belongings, folks around the office were talking about the impressive buyout she had been offered. No one knew the exact figure, which left everyone free to speculate on just how much it might be. Amounts were floated, neither confirmed nor denied. By the third time I heard the rumors, roughly an hour after they began, the handsome sum had grown into an awesomely huge amount of money. Each time the rumor made its way back to me, I'd add an additional 10 percent before passing it on. Then I would sit back and wait with anticipation to hear how much more the amount grew during its journey through the next round of the rumor mill.

And grow it did.

Within days, people were claiming that she got enough money to afford a second home in Florida. Within a week, with a little help from me, the office scuttlebutt had her relocating full time to Paris.

Secretly, everyone was cheering for her. We all wanted to believe that she wasn't crazy but rather that she really wanted a buyout and was clever enough to get it. Somehow it gave us hope.

This happened many years ago, but I will admit that on really tough days at the office, my thoughts drift back to this fine woman and her remarkable exit strategy. It is not that I dislike my work. In fact, I'm very fortunate to have had an interesting and rewarding career. But even the best jobs come with those days when you are tired of the tasks, fed up with the bureaucracy and longing to do something different. And as the years have passed, those days seem to come with increasing frequency. For a long time, I thought there was little I could do about it, being too young to retire and too old to get a new job. Yet, inspired by Susan, I began to wonder if I, too, could come up with a crazy idea just sane enough to get me that coveted buyout. I realized right away that any effective idea would have to meet two critical criteria:

Creepy. It would have to be something that would make people think twice about my overall mental health but without being truly dangerous.

Legal: Whatever the idea, it had to be legal—well within the bounds of my rights as an individual, regardless of how weird or off-putting.

I cycled through a lot of seemingly good ideas. One of the first was to get prison-like tattoos where the knuckles on one hand would read "HATE" and on the other hand "WORK." I could envision myself sitting in meetings with my hands clenched and resting prominently in front of me, occasionally pounding them on the table to make a point or just to draw attention.

I toyed with becoming an Über Christian—beginning each meeting with a prayer, ending every conversation with a "God bless you and your family," and maybe even forming a lunchtime prayer group. I gave up on this idea when I realized that it might require me to actually learn something about the Bible. This seemed like far too much work.

Continuous drooling was my next idea, followed by uncontrollable flatulence. Both had their merits. Even if they did not result in me being offered money to leave, I most certainly would be invited to far fewer meetings and that alone might be worth the effort. I ran the drooling idea past my wife, Sylvia. She shot it down. She said it would make me look unattractive. I decided she was right. I'm already a little challenged in the appearance area and don't need to make matters worse.

Flatulence was more complicated. I couldn't figure out how to cause it, at least not on the scale I was looking for. If I was going to do this, I wanted to be able to fill rooms, if not entire floors, with my special aroma. Eventually I flushed this idea down the crapper, so to speak.

One idea I really liked was to start talking to myself in whispers while sitting in meetings, riding the elevator or passing people in the hall. To ratchet up the level of creepiness, these conversations would be designed to lead others to think I was developing a severe multiple personality disorder, with one of my personas clearly exhibiting a hostile attitude toward the other. I could envision myself and I arguing over simple things like where to have lunch, then taking it up a notch as we fought over who was responsible for screwing up a project, and finally finishing off with a screaming match over which of us Mom and Dad liked better and why. In the end I dropped this idea when I realized that someone in the office was already doing a version of it and, as yet, had been unsuccessful in getting a buyout offer.

Then one day I was driving to work when a "touron" (what Washington, D.C. residents call a combination of tourist and moron) from Indiana made a right turn from the far-left lane, nearly plowing into my car as he did. My response was completely unexpected. I started barking. I'm not talking about a friendly Shitzu or Yorkie bark. My bark was more like that of a pit bull on steroids. The touron never heard me. He was driving too fast. But I felt surprisingly better. I had let something primeval loose. From that moment on, I continued to bark whenever another driver did something monumentally stupid. Sometimes I'd mimic the growl of a German Shepherd warning off a rival. Other times I'd go for the vicious bark of a junkyard dog straining at the end of his chain. I began to wonder if maybe it was time to take barking to the office. I could picture myself sitting in meetings with my fellow managers and howling at anyone who said anything idiotic or just doing a low growl if anyone came close to the edge of stupidity. This was a surefire idea. The only danger would be that others might catch on and start barking back. And while contemplating how I would respond to that potential situation, I was struck, out of the blue, with ...

The ultimate idea!

The absolutely perfect idea! One that met all the requirements of being both creepy (to the max) and perfectly legal. An idea so simple that half the people on the planet could do it and so perfect as to amaze me that it had never been done before. An idea that can be summed up in two words—Hitler Mustache. I WOULD GROW A HITLER MUSTACHE! When you think about it, what could possibly be wrong with that? After all, it's been 70+ years since Hitler died. Should a whole grooming option for men be condemned for eternity just because one really bad guy adopted it? YES, of course it should be condemned for eternity, because the Hitler mustache is a symbol of evil. It outpolls Lucifer's horns, KKK robes and Dick Cheney's face as one of the most singularly disturbing symbols of evil ever. That is why it's perfect. No office anywhere, in any country, or on this planet or any other planet, is going to want an employee with a Hitler mustache. Yet, you can't be fired for it. It's a personal grooming choice—one that is guaranteed to elicit that prized buyout offer.

The only problem? I couldn't bring myself to do it.

I'll admit I had some concerns about riding the subway with a Hitler mustache. It's the sort of thing that makes you stand out even if you're in a car with a half-naked guy who is peeing himself. But I could deal with that. Besides, how long would it take for my employer to cave? A day? Maybe two? This was the perfect idea.

In fact, all my exit strategies were good. But I just couldn't pull the trigger on any of them, and I couldn't figure out why.

After a lot of soul searching, it finally hit me. I was petrified by the thought of retirement, scared to death, even if it came with a big fat check to leave. Work had become an enormous part of my life, the source of much of my self-worth and one of my few links to a community of people who (mostly) share the same goals.

I have spent so many years working, I wasn't sure I would know how not to work. With the advent of email and cell phones and Internet, my job had expanded to 50 or 60 hours a week. The hobbies and interests of my youth had fallen by the wayside. Even once-treasured vacations stopped being real vacations when the expectation became that we would carry our smartphones wherever we went.

Like all people contemplating retirement, I worried about the money. But after a very fortunate career, I could afford it. No, what really worried me was time.

How would I fill my days? What would I do for fun? How would I find meaning in my life? How would I avoid succumbing to a retirement spent largely in front of a TV?

On the surface, retirement looks great. It's a chance to do all the things I've never done before like jump out of an airplane, or run with the bulls in Spain, or sail around the world or climb Mount Everest. But the truth is I've never really wanted to do any of these things. Risking my life does not strike me as fun.

Yet I know there must be things I would enjoy doing, ways to get the most out of what retirement offers. That's when I decided I needed to reconnect with the hobbies I used to love when I was younger and find new and exciting activities to pursue. I needed ways to express my creativity and connect with communities of other retirees who share similar interests.

So, about a year before my anticipated retirement, I made a commitment to myself and Sylvia to stop with the 50- to 60-hour work weeks, to adopt a more normal work schedule and to devote the extra time to seeking new adventures.

This book chronicles my journey over the course of one year, 2016, into the unknown world of excess time, limited responsibilities and an uncertain future. I hope my adventures can help others who are about to embark down the same path.

Ball challenged

I am ball challenged.

It doesn't matter whether it's a ball you hit, catch, dribble, shoot, throw, bounce, serve, dodge, return, kick or roll. Big balls or small balls, size doesn't matter either. What they all have in common is this: They don't like me.

As a kid, my version of kickball rarely involved kicking the ball. Basketball was devoid of baskets. In baseball, my best hope of getting on base was to get hit by the ball. And, as you can probably surmise, I also sucked at dodge ball.

So it will come as no surprise that I grew up never fully understanding the fascination with ball-related sports. People will pay good money and spend hours of their time to watch teams of people fight to move a ball from one side of a field or court to another. They will settle in for entire weekends in front of the TV watching baseball, football, basketball, tennis or soccer on any one of the countless stations dedicated to sports. This ball fascination is so ingrained in our culture that men have come to routinely refer to their genitals as "balls," even though they are actually more oblong than round* and even though, as all men would agree, they should never be hit, caught, dribbled, shot, thrown, bounced, served, dodged, returned, kicked or rolled.

But there is one sport involving a ball that has always intrigued me—golf.

Based on its staying power alone, there must be something to this sport. The oldest references to any golf-like game date back to the early 14th century, with the earliest course dating to 1389. (Historical note: no Blacks, Jews or women allowed.) The first shipment of clubs arrived in the New World in 1739, no doubt destined for some early colonial banker, insurance salesman, doctor or hedge fund manager. Today an estimated 24 million Americans play golf and spend $27 billion a year to do so. That's ten times what we spend on toilet paper each year and three times more than we spend on beer—and those are necessities. These are not made-up facts.

To be honest, though, there is more to the story concerning my fascination with golf. For me, it is the forbidden fruit of all sports. This goes back to my childhood. When I was 12, my father sat me down to tell me the facts of life. This was the conversation I was waiting for, when the mysteries of life would be revealed—when I would finally find out the purpose behind my personal set of balls. I was anxious. I was ready. I was focused. I sat on the edge of the sofa while my dad settled into his recliner and cracked open a beer. He held the can against his lips, slowly tipping it back to take a drink that seemed to go on forever.

Finally, he looked at me and said, "Son, there are two types of people in the world, bowlers and golfers. We're bowlers." A long, awkward silence hung between us while I took this in. What the hell did he mean? Was it a complex metaphor for sex? Was he saying that bowlers got all the girls and if I took up bowling I could look forward to a lifetime of incredible satisfaction with any number of beautiful young ladies? Then it occurred to me that maybe he was saying just the opposite. Maybe this was his way of telling me all the beautiful girls were golfing and I would be condemned to spend my life in the bowling alley.

I thought long and hard about what he had said. Days went by, then weeks, in which I thought of little else. Then it eventually hit me—the sudden realization that like so many other words of wisdom he had passed down to me, I had no idea what he was talking about. But clearly golf was somehow a far more important and complex topic than sex.

Fifty years later, I find myself writing a book on things to do in retirement. There is no way I can leave out the No. 1 retirement activity next to watching daytime TV, complaining about children, bragging about grandchildren and discussing medical ailments. I finally had to unravel the mysteries of golf for myself. I signed up for Golf 101 at a local public golf course. The class met every Saturday morning for five weeks.

While driving to the course for the first time, a horrible thought crossed my mind: What if I turn out to be really good at this? What if I turn out to be a natural born golfer? What if I were one of those one-in-a-hundred-million babies with just the right mix of DNA to guarantee the massive wealth and low-stress life of a golf pro, destined to travel the world visiting beautiful courses, playing a game all day, hanging out in clubhouses and making millions of dollars? Maybe that could have been me. I could have been rich. Maybe even rich enough to have challenged Tiger Woods' record for the most high-priced prostitutes slept with in a single night. But none of this could possibly happen now because I had taken up the game too late! Would I be able to handle the anger and depression of knowing that my life could have been so different if only my dad had said, "We're golfers, not bowlers." Could I ever come to terms with the obvious betrayal by my own father?

Without getting too far ahead of the story, these fears turned out to be completely unfounded.

Lesson One was all about putting. I teamed up with Britney, a woman in her early 20s who was learning to golf because her boyfriend was "totally" into the game. Britney was very nice and I liked her. She laughed at my jokes. Britney either has a great sense of humor or is exceedingly polite. We practiced putting for about an hour. I would like to say that I sank three consecutive 20-foot puts. Saying that, however, would be a complete and total lie. I did sink several two- to three-foot putts, but probably missed ten times as many from the same distances.

The next week's class focused on chipping. Using an eight iron, we learned how to get off the rough and onto the green. The best part, though, was getting to drive the cart. At first, I insisted that Britney take the wheel. I didn't want to come off like a sexist old fart. Britney won my heart by suggesting we take turns. The cart's top speed was 10 miles an hour, but that didn't matter. It was fun to open the throttle and take the tight turns of the cart path. This was topped only by off-roading on the fairways, a cool ride where Britney and I would try to go as fast as we could while avoiding the sand traps along the way.

A few days later I was back at the golf course getting in some practice between lessons. I placed the ball in the rough about two yards from the edge of the green and a total of 25 feet from the cup. I brought my club back a foot or so and took the shot. The ball took flight, gathering just enough initial altitude to clear a slight incline before reaching the peak of its arch about four feet off the ground. The ball then began to descend, hitting the green about a third of the way to the cup. It bounced several times before gracefully rolling in a straight line that would take it about a foot and a half to the left of the flag. As the ball got closer its speed began to diminish. It then did something I had hoped for but never really expected—the ball, following the contour of the green, headed directly for the cup. As it reached the edge of the hole, it seemed to lose the last bit of its momentum. It stopped for just a second, just long enough to look back at me and smile, before rolling over the edge. That moment, the very instant the ball dropped in the cup, I understood the insidious nature of golf. This was a game that provided players with just enough reward to keep them going. For an hour or more before this beautiful shot, I'd struggled to get the ball to do anything. I hit countless shots where the ball rolled completely across the green and into the rough on the other side. I took a few shots where the ball moved no more than a foot or two. I overcompensated for these, at one point hitting the ball so hard that it traveled through the air like a line drive, passing just a foot or two to the left of another golfer. This resulted in the kind of verbal exchange you don't expect to hear on a golf course and that no amount of apologizing on my part could seem to tamper.

Yet every bad shot was quickly forgotten in that one instant when I watched the ball leave my club and travel 25 perfect feet into the cup. Clearly, I had done something right. And if I could do that once, I could surely do it again and then again after that, right? And for the next 30 minutes I tried and failed to prove this hypothesis. Eventually I hit a ball from the rough that rolled to within a foot of the hole. Did I get it in the cup? No. But close enough. I declared victory and was not about to press my luck. I immediately packed up to go home. It was best to leave on a high note.

Lessons Three and Four drove home all the points learned during practice. The only consistency I had was the ability to hit the occasionally beautiful shot that would make me briefly forget the absolutely maddening, frustrating aspects of golf. At one point, our class was teeing off on the driving range. I managed to hit four good shots straight down the fairway. I was feeling good. I was feeling confident. I was becoming a real golfer. I decided to go for the gold and give it my all. This turned out to be a big mistake.

Some say it is impossible to hit a ball that will travel at a perfect 90-degree angle to the club. I proved them wrong. I watched in horror as the shot took to the sky, veering radically to the right and leaving the driving range altogether. It eventually returned to earth, landing directly in front of a golf cart driven by an elderly woman who, along with her presumed husband, were just out for a Saturday morning drive to the first tee. They seemed a bit surprised by the unexpected intruder and immediately looked around to see where it might have come from. I, however, not wishing to be reported to the golf course's upper management, shifted my gaze from their cart to the fairway. I put my hand to the brim of my cap as if my eyes were following an imaginary ball that traveled at least 150 yards down the driving range. I then immediately teed up the next shot. There were a lot of players on the driving range that day. There was no way they could pin this on me. Some lessons you learn from golf have less to do with the game and more to do with basic survival. And some lessons you learn about survival from more than 40 years of working can be applied anywhere they are needed.

Our final lesson added a whole new element—public humiliation. The class played two holes together in weather so bad it reminded me of the scene from Caddyshack in which Bill Murray carries a set of clubs for the local bishop. The only difference is that in the movie the bishop was having the game of his soon-to-be-over life, hitting one terrific shot after another. I, on the other hand, was teeing up in front of the whole class. I didn't feel comfortable having an audience and it showed. The best shot I had all morning involved driving a clump of grass ten yards straight down the fairway. It was, sadly, the only shot I had all day that hadn't sliced frighteningly to the right.

I wanted to play the clump where it landed. The instructor insisted I play with an actual golf ball. He asked me to try again. I complied, sending a shot off the 18th tee that headed toward the 17th fairway. Other than the clump of grass, it was the best shot I had all day.

Eventually the lesson was over; in fact, all five were. What did I learn? I found golf frustrating, maddening and humiliating—but also challenging and, honestly, a lot of fun as long as you don't care how well you're playing. I've come to understand why people like the game. After five lessons, I realize that with a lot of effort, I could probably be good at it. No Tiger Woods, but good enough to get together with a group of people and spend an afternoon walking around a beautiful golf course, honing my skills, enjoying pleasant conversation and getting a little exercise. All and all, not a bad way to spend an afternoon if you are retired. So, when my instructor suggested I consider signing up for Golf 102, I jumped at the chance. Look for more on Golf 102 in the sequel to this book!

As I wrote this I realized that just because my balls are more oblong than round doesn't mean that all men's balls are more oblong than round. Maybe most men do have round balls? Mine could be a genetic mutation, something outside the norm but far superior, no doubt, to those of other men with the more common round balls. I had no way of knowing—no real frame of reference for comparing my genitalia with those of other men. So I decided to Google it and according to my extensive three-minute Internet research on men's balls, they are normally egg-shaped. Which proved my point. Why do we call them balls when they are really egg-shaped? Damn ball culture. (Of note: I also learned from Google that it is common for the left ball to hang lower than the right one. This is a relief to know. Thanks, Google!)

Cooking up romance

Everything I know about cooking I learned from my mom. She put the best of her skills into every meal she made. Each dish helped shape my understanding of the vast, complex flavors of food. Every entry built upon the one before, refining my palate and developing within me a set of beliefs about the nature of food and fine dining that I carried into my adult life.

The only problem? My mom is a terrible cook. Just horrible. Most meals in our home were so bad that even the dog turned up his nose at the leftovers. He supplemented his normal diet of dry cubes of off-brand dog chow by going door to door throughout the neighborhood begging for edible leftovers. My sisters and I admired his entrepreneurial spirit, but mostly we envied his success. He would carry home the fruits of his labor (rarely fruit) to parade in front of us, always adding a low growl to make sure we understood he was the alpha dog and would not be sharing no matter how much we begged.

As a result of these early dining experiences, the perspective on food I developed as a child turned out to be, well, forgive me Mom, a little skewed. A few examples to illustrate:

- I was in my early teens before I realized that spinach was, in fact, a leafy vegetable that didn't naturally emerge from the earth as a frozen brick of green slime that had to be boiled for several hours into a stringy pea-soup-like mash before it could be consumed. As a small child, I was told by my mom that spinach was grown at the North Pole by Santa's elves during the off-season. I believed her. I could picture Rudolf and his friends pulling the plow as the elves toiled through thick layers of ice to plant their precious spinach seeds in the cold, hard ground. I often wondered if they knew how much I hated spinach and how little I appreciated their efforts.

- I labored for years under the conviction that Velveeta was real cheese, that orange was the natural color of all cheeses and that any cheese that was not orange was just trying to pass itself off as something it was not—some kind of cheese wanna-be. I furthermore believed that all real cheeses (i.e., Velveeta) were best served on Wonder bread with lots of mayonnaise and garnished with a side of Kraft Mac and Cheese (orange cheese in powder form).

- I was convinced that salt and pepper were the only true spices and certainly the only spices that anyone would ever need. Ketchup was a close second (or third, depending on how you count). Although not technically a spice, it was treated as such in my family and probably most families at the time. Ketchup is marvelous —a miracle blend of tomatoes, processed oils and refined white sugar that you can put on any food to hide its flavor. This was especially useful when it came to Mrs. Paul's Frozen Fish Sticks, which my mom baked every Friday night as part of her never-ending quest to honor her Catholic roots by torturing her children.

Knowing all this, you may be surprised to learn that when Sylvia and I got married, I became the cook in our home. I did not do this willingly. I caved under protest, mostly out of desperation.

Early in our marriage I came to the realization that if I didn't cook, we didn't eat. I tested this theory and found that Sylvia could go days, possibly weeks, without eating. She could go so long without food that I began to wonder if eating was really a necessity for any of us. I started imagining a world in which none of God's creatures had to eat—a world where every living thing could survive on nothing but water and air. What an incredible world that would be! All of God's creatures living in harmony, where a lion could lie down with a lamb, where a man could hug a Great White shark with no fear of being eaten, and where even Israelis and Palestinians would embrace as brothers before annihilating each other in a hail of gunfire and exploding suicide vests. This would be a perfect world. There would be no starvation. No competing for scarce resources. Just a whole bunch of people sitting around in harmony taking deep breaths, drinking lots of water and fornicating as often as they wanted.

I knew right away that I was onto something. I was on the verge of an epiphany, an entirely new way of looking at the world and the nature of our relationship with God—an insight so powerful that I might emerge as the next prophet, a Moses or Muhammad or, at least, a David Koresh or Jim Jones. But by this time, though, I'd gone so long without food that my stomach started churning. And the closer I came to this grand revelation about God, Man and the Universe, the louder my stomach grew until finally I became so distracted that I lost my train of thought.

The meaning of life had slipped through my grasp. I was disappointed. Depressed. So I went to the refrigerator and made a Velveeta sandwich on Wonder bread with lots of mayonnaise. I felt better.

But enough about God. Let's get back to the important things in life, like food.

Armed with my mom's wedding gift, her 1952 copy of the Betty Crocker Cookbook, I was ready to take on the role of chef in our home. I stocked up on all the recommended basic supplies: Sugar, salt, butter, flour and of course Crisco, the miracle ingredient of my childhood. You could make pie crusts with it, fry steaks in it, spread it on white bread and eat it as a sandwich or just lick it off a spoon. I still keep a few tubs hidden in the basement just in case the zombie apocalypse turns out to be more than just a social media rumor.

After Sylvia and I got married, we tried preparing meals together. That didn't last long. I have been accused of being a control freak. This is because I am a complete and unrepentant control freak. In my world, there is no task too small not to be added to a to-do list; no line, whether at a bank, airport or supermarket, that could not benefit from a few helpful suggestions about how to form a more perfect queue; and, no problem, no matter how inconsequential, that cannot and should not interfere with any chance of getting a good night's sleep. This highly valued asset during my years of working is not always appreciated at home. Perfectly valid criticism about how someone (I won't name names) is chopping onions can be met with hostility even if combined with helpful suggestions on how to do it right. For the sake of our marriage, a division of labor was needed. For that, we turned to the Old Testament, the Book of Leviticus #113:

He who shall cooketh the evening meal, shall not be expected to loadeth the dishwasher or wipeth down the counters.

She who shall not cooketh the meal but who shall partake in its bounty shall be responsible for all cleaning associated with the preparation of the harvest provided by the Lord.

Peace has reigned in our home for more than 30 years.

I would like to say that over the course of our marriage I've become pretty good at cooking, but that would be a stretch. The best I can say is that I am okay at it. Sylvia rarely complains about what I serve, and our former dog was an enthusiastic consumer of all food that dropped on the floor. Admittedly, he may not have been the best judge of quality. He was also known to eat string, plastic bottle caps and the edges of rugs.

Over the years, I've had just enough success in the kitchen to convince me that I can do better. Knowing that retirement will provide me with ample opportunity to step up my game, I decided to take a cooking class.

Much to my delight, when I Googled cooking classes in the Washington, D.C., area, hundreds of results popped up. Choosing among the offerings was not easy. Fortunately, a retired friend came to the rescue. He recommended a culinary school not far from our house. He cautioned me, however, to be wary of the middle-aged, recently divorced women who, he said, made up most of his class. He claimed to have had to fend off more than one unexpected advance. This concerned me. I am deeply, madly and passionately in love with my wife and have never strayed. I would like to attribute this to my incredible willpower (making sure my upper brain always dominates my lower brain). However, I also recognize that I'm rarely in a situation where there might be a lot of women throwing themselves at me. (Did I just write "rarely" in the last sentence? Let's go with full disclosure: I have never been in any situation where women were throwing themselves at me. Hence the concern.) Nevertheless, and armed with this note of caution, I decided to go through with my plans.

Taking cooking classes with Sylvia was the obvious solution for keeping other women at bay. Truthfully, though, she was not my first choice. I had serious reservations about violating our 30-year agreement covering food preparation. Second only to our wedding vows, this unwritten contract has served as a cornerstone of our marriage. Only after exhausting my entire Rolodex of apparently very busy friends did I decide that maybe it was time for us to try teamwork.

This left just one last decision: Which class would we take? French cuisine? Mexican? Peruvian? Asian? While I initially wanted to sign up for "Pork-a-licious" or "Knife Etiquette," we ended up going with Asian cooking. We chose this option largely because, with a little whining on my part, Sylvia finally agreed that she would go with me but only if I picked Asian cooking.

The class met for three hours on a Saturday afternoon. There were about 20 students ranging from several newly married couples to a woman in her 80s and her 50ish daughter who dressed in matching outfits —white and red striped shirts, white slacks and matching brown shoes. I have no idea why and I was afraid to I ask. It was one of those situations where you know that whatever the answer is, it's going to be weird. There were also some single guys who did not appear to be a couple. And none of these people—

nobody—resembled the desperate divorcees my friend had warned me about.

We focused on making five dishes, starting with a chicken curry soup, moving next to a shrimp-based Thai dish, then a Korean beef dish with baby bok choy on the side, and finishing with sweet sticky rice.

To my relief, Sylvia and I developed a good rhythm for food preparation. We divided all food chopping equally (except for the onions, which I did). She handled all grating because it seemed that whenever I tried to grate anything, it ended up on the floor. While I routinely practice the three-second rule at home, Sylvia was vehemently opposed to me doing this in front of strangers. Despite this minor disagreement, everything went smoothly for the first hour or so. Then my wife left the safety of our food station to take several cubed pieces of tofu to be deep fried before being added to the chicken curry soup. I remained back at the table chopping lemon grass. As Sylvia lined up for the deep fryer, I noticed that one of the single guys who had been circulating around the edges of the herd suddenly got in line right behind her. He was young, probably no more than 53, with the kind of good looks I assumed made up for a complete lack of personality. Apparently, this was not the case, though, as he seemed quite agile in striking up a conversation with the woman I love. I watched as they chatted, both smiling and even laughing. I thought about walking over with my rather long, rather sharp knife and going all Jeffrey Dahmer on him but decided against it. I knew Sylvia could take care of herself.

Eventually my beloved made it back to our prep station with the deep-fried tofu, the last but essential ingredient for the soup. The young man who was hitting on her went his own way. I kept the knife handy just in case he circled back.

So, what did we learn from this cooking class? Except for the soup and the dessert, I realized that what good Asian cooking comes down to is sauces. We made some terrific marinades of soy sauce, oyster and fish sauce, sugar, garlic, curry chili paste and a host of other ingredients which have now become staples in our house. I've become convinced that a good sauce will make just about any kind of meat taste great.

I also learned that if you are a man or woman of a certain age and find yourself suddenly single, taking a cooking course or two might not be a bad way of meeting someone. Just keep in mind that in any good cooking class, there may be a few husbands or wives you weren't aware of and there are a lot of very sharp knives within easy reach.

Yoga makes
me sick

For years, Sylvia has been pestering me to take up yoga. She brings it up all the time. She says it's good exercise. She claims it will help me relax.

Here's why I initially resisted:

What is yoga?

Is it exercise or relaxation? It can't be both. Exercise is when I get on the stationary bike and strenuously pedal in place going nowhere for 30 minutes while sweat pours off my body, soaking through my underwear and, in the process, producing a level of body odor that even I find disgusting. I work out three or four times a week. By the time I'm done my body is producing so much perspiration that I'm like a walking river. If I stand in one place too long, I produce a lake. That's what I consider exercise.

Relaxation, on the other hand, comes hours later when I kick back in the Lay-Z-Boy, turn on the TV and crack open a beer or two. I have no interest in combining the two into some kind of new-age journey of self-discovery.

What are the positions?

The only yoga position I know is the Lotus position. That's where you sit on the floor with your legs crossed and your feet twisted into a pretzel so that your ankles rest on your inner thighs. I couldn't sit like this when I was 6 years old and I sure as hell can't do it now. And even if I could get into that position, I'm not sure I'd want to. At my age I fear getting stuck and having to have the paramedics break my legs to set me free.

What to wear?

I envisioned yoga classes being populated by lots of people wearing spandex. I have nothing against spandex, but I do strongly support the belief that no one over 40 should wear it. I'll be the first to admit that on the right person, spandex can be a thing of beauty—gently caressing every lovely curve of a well-toned body. However, on the not-so-well-toned body, spandex can apply its same magical properties to accent every pound of excess weight, making each ounce look like an undulating mountain of fat. This is the category I fall into. Spandex is out. A friend told me you can wear whatever is comfortable to a yoga class, even shorts. That notion horrifies me. I prefer boxer shorts to briefs. I'm uncomfortable with the idea that I could find myself stretched out in some weird yoga position with my butt over my head and my junk clearly exposed to anyone looking down the leg of my shorts.

Yet, I had to admit that Sylvia may have had a point. Relaxation does not come naturally to me. Worrying does. Give my brain a few minutes of unsupervised free time and it is remarkable how quickly it will wander off to things like house fires (did I turn off the stove?), potential stock market collapses (do I have the proper asset allocation?) and cancer (yes, that thing on my forehead did turn out to be skin cancer but not the bad kind). And that's just the warm-up! Given enough time, my brain can conjure up every embarrassing moment in my life, and when it runs out of things there, it will start cycling through bad experiences from other people's lives.

As a result, I have found that the key to happiness is to keep my brain busy. Constantly busy. This requires me to think all the time—especially to think up things that will keep me from thinking about the things I really don't want to think about. This is exhausting. That's why I started to consider that Sylvia might have a point.

It wasn't Sylvia, however, who ultimately persuaded me to try yoga. It was my cat, Portia.

I envy Portia. She doesn't worry about anything. This may be true of all cats. It's certainly not true about dogs. Leave a dog at home when you go to work and it will worry all day about whether you're ever coming back. And then when you do return, the poor dog is so relieved to find out he hasn't been abandoned that he almost has a heart attack letting you know how happy he is to see you.

Portia is extremely affectionate but could not care less if I leave the house. She never worries about whether I'm coming back. She never thinks twice about where her next meal is coming from. She doesn't concern herself with paying bills, growing old or whether some of her cells have begun to multiply in erratic and unhealthy ways.

To her way of thinking, she is a goddess. She has two human slaves to take care of all her needs and owns a nice house that is no doubt paid for from the sale of her incredibly valuable poop that Sylvia and I harvest each night from her litter boxes. This frees her up to spend most of her time seeking the ultimate Zen-like state of relaxation. Sometimes this involves hours of lying in the same position on our bed. Other times it requires her to relocate, following the sun as it moves from one room to the next.

I've studied her behavior and I can't help but notice that when she does move, it always starts with a large yawn followed by extending her front legs as far as she can. Then she'll stretch her back legs, slowly opening and closing her paws each time. When that is done, she works her way onto all fours and arches her back while twisting her shoulders from side to side. Only then, after this careful ritual, will she take a step forward and sometimes not even then. Sometimes she'll go through the motions of getting up only to lie back down and go to sleep. God I envy her.

I realized one day while watching her that what she was doing looked like some form of cat yoga. And it seems to work. She is always at peace with the world and always in a state of bliss.

I ran this "cat yoga" revelation by Sylvia, who reminded me, yet again, in what is starting to become a recurring theme, that I am "not allowed to get any weirder." However, after discussing it a bit, she seemed to come around and was eventually pleased that I was opening to the idea of yoga. She even sweetened the deal by offering to go with me.

I was not ready to commit. Not yet. If I was going to do this, I needed to know more about yoga. Research was key.

Whenever I'm faced with a perplexing question, I turn to the one source I can trust for accurate answers: the Internet. So, I booted up my PC, waited the required 20 minutes for Windows to load, connected to the web, opened Google and typed "yoga" into the search option.

Google returned 313,000,000 matches.

This seems like a lot. It's almost as many hits as there are people in the United States. I was amazed. The results were so numerous that even Google was rounding off—and not to the nearest hundred or thousand or even hundred thousand but to the nearest million. This got me wondering. How does Google rank all these results? How does it determine what goes on top of the list and what sinks to the bottom? And what about that last item? What could possibly be just relevant enough to Google's search algorithm to be included in the results but so minimally important and tenuously tied to the subject as to come up last in a list of 313,000,000 results? I contemplated scrolling through every page to get to the last one but realized that this would probably take a decade or longer so I opted instead to open the first match on the list—Wikipedia. In retrospect, this may not have been the best selection.

Here's some of what Wikipedia had to say about the meaning of yoga:

Yoga can take on meanings such as "connection", "contact", "union", "method", "application", "addition" and "performance". In simpler words, Yoga also means "combined". For example, guṇáyoga means "contact with a cord"; chakráyoga has a medical sense of "applying a splint or similar instrument by means of pulleys (in case of dislocation of the thigh)"; chandráyoga has the astronomical sense of "conjunction of the moon with a constellation"; puṃyoga is a grammatical term expressing "connection or relation with a man", etc.

This was followed by Wikipedia's explanation of several types of yoga, including things like this:

Ashtanga Yoga incorporates epistemology, metaphysics, ethical practices, systematic exercises and self-development techniques for body, mind and spirit. Its epistemology (pramanas) is same as the Samkhya school. Both accept three reliable means to knowledge – perception (pratyākṣa, direct sensory observations), inference (anumāna) and testimony of

40

trustworthy experts (sabda, agama). Both these orthodox schools are also strongly dualistic.

Then there was this paragraph on yoga's history:

Onesicritus also mentions his colleague Calanus trying to meet them, who is initially denied audience, but later invited because he was sent by a "king curious of wisdom and philosophy". Onesicritus and Calanus learn that the yogins consider the best doctrine of life as "rid the spirit of not only pain, but also pleasure", that "man trains the body for toil in order that his opinions may be strengthened", that "there is no shame in life on frugal fare", and that "the best place to inhabit is one with scantiest equipment or outfit". These principles are significant to the history of spiritual side of yoga.

Let me cut to the chase. Yoga may bring enlightenment but Wikipedia sure as hell didn't. Yes, I discovered that there is a spiritual aspect to yoga, which I think I already knew. It was also clear yoga has been around awhile, although exactly how long I was not sure. And I came to understand that there are different kinds of yoga. But come on, Wikipedia! Simple English, please! I've reviewed legal contracts that are easier to read.

Recognizing that Wikipedia had failed me, I tried a second search: "types of yoga." Google returned 20 million hits. I started at the top. The first link identified 16 kinds of yoga. The next listed nine.

41

The third, six. I reviewed them all trying to decide which was right for me.

Acro Yoga, I learned, "helps students learn how to fly." I was a little skeptical of this. If it were true, I would surely have encountered at least one of my fellow commuters flying to work Superman style rather than sitting in traffic next to me while we all cursed the unknown idiot who was holding everything up. Acro Yoga failed my credibility test. It was out.

Ashtanga Yoga was described as "intensively physically demanding." I crossed it off my list. Dropping dead from a heart attack in front of a room full of strangers on my first day of yoga would be too embarrassing.

Hot Yoga was intriguing. This is where you do yoga in a room heated to 105 degrees Fahrenheit. The article promised it would "help you sweat out toxins while you work toward increased strength and flexibility." I eventually decided against it because I like my toxins. They may not be good for me, but they are mine and we have learned to live together in harmony. I am not going to risk upsetting an already delicate interpersonal relationship.

I also decided against Prenatal Yoga for obvious reasons.

I seriously considered Yin Yoga because it has a catchy, lyrical name and promised to involve a lot of sitting. Sitting is good.

Then I discovered the following write-up for Tantra Yoga: "While most of us think of sex when we think of Tantra Yoga, this ancient practice is actually a powerful combination of asana, mantra, mudra, and bandha (energy lock) and chakra (energy center) that you can use to build strength, clarity, and bliss in everyday life." Further research uncovered a site that described Tantra yoga as "definitely orgasmic but not sexual." To be honest, I'd never heard of Tantra Yoga and had no idea what asana, mantra, mudra, bandha or chakra are, but I didn't need to know any of this. They had me at the sex. I needed to find out how something could be orgasmic but not sexual.

With the type of yoga firmly decided I still had that pesky issue of what to wear. I went back to the Google for a search on "yoga clothes."

Google returned 21,600,000 hits. At this point, I was beginning to think Google was just toying with me. I mean, really! 21,600,000 hits. How is this even remotely possible? Is there some kind of government regulation that requires manufacturers to create a web page for each article of clothing they make? I didn't know. I didn't care and I was absolutely not going to go through all of them. So instead I started with the first option that popped up: Lululemon. I immediately took a liking to this company because of their slogan: "Our Yoga gear is Down Dog approved." I was intrigued by the idea of a pet-friendly company, especially one that employed a canine approval squad. I could picture a pack of German shepherds sniffing each article of clothing as it came off the line. I could imagine them going on breaks together, hanging out after work, maybe starting a bowling team or a mutual butt-sniffing society. Unfortunately, though, Lululemon turned out to carry clothes only for women. I moved on. I was going to try the next site, Beyond

Yoga, but I skipped it. I figured that you actually have to do yoga before going "beyond" yoga. I didn't want to look like a pretentious asshole at my first class showing up in some super high-end yoga clothes, especially since I was likely to demonstrate to everyone that I hadn't the slightest idea what I was doing. Fabletics was next. It had the best-looking models by far but the longer I stayed on the site, the more I felt like some kind of 60-year-old pervert. Several times I had to stop and ask myself if I was shopping or gawking. After a couple of hours without making an actual purchase, the answer was obvious. With regret, I finally went to Amazon and in no time had narrowed my options to two: a pair of sweatpants that ended at the knees or some spandex-like underwear designed to be worn under shorts. I bought them both.

The final challenge was finding a yoga studio. This was easy. I picked the one closest to my house. The young lady who answered the phone was very helpful. I asked about Tantra Yoga but she politely explained that they didn't offer it. I was disappointed. I didn't have a Plan B. Yet I had come so far and I was determined not to give up. After explaining my full situation, the young woman recommended a type of yoga she referred to as "be-gin-ner" yoga. I couldn't recall this "be-gin-ner" yoga coming up in any of my Google searches, but had to remind myself that I hadn't gone through all 20 million hits. It didn't matter, though. At this point, I decided to put my trust in the hands of the young professional on the other end of the line. I signed myself and Sylvia up for three lessons for $33 each. A reasonable price, I thought.

When the big day came, my dear wife bailed on me. She claimed to have a good reason—something about "not feeling well." She may have been faking it, but I was committed.

Before leaving the house, I debated as to which of my new yoga outfits to wear and settled on the knee-length sweatpants and a loose-fitting T-shirt. I checked myself out in the mirror. I looked quite sporting, like a 60-year-old homeless guy in ill-fitting sweatpants and a baggy 10-year-old T-shirt.

Class began with us all lying on our backs while the lights were dimmed and the yoga instructor read a spiritual poem to help connect us to the larger universe around us. I felt relaxed. I was already starting to like yoga but then, just as I was about to nod off, the poetry ended and the movement began.

Yoga, I quickly discovered, is about gentle, fluid motion—slowly stretching, smoothly extending the arms and legs, bringing them together and then extending them again.

That is not exactly how it worked for me. My body moved with all the grace and smoothness of C3PO from the original Star Wars. At one point, I extended forward, putting most of my weight on one knee and then holding the position. This resulted in some major-league leg muscle twitching, making me wonder if I might have to be checked out for Parkinson's disease. Fortunately, as I was obsessing on that horrible thought, my foot cramped up. The pain from that was enough to drive away the thoughts of Parkinson's disease.

For those thinking about taking a yoga class, I would suggest spending a little time learning a couple of the basic positions. I didn't bother to do that. While the instructor was very good about describing positions like Warrior 1, Warrior 2 and Downward-facing dog, she was a little hard to follow. Fortunately, the 70-something woman next to me wearing tight black Spandex (and, I might add, pulling it off) knew all the moves. I kept my eyes on her and followed everything she did. By the end of the class I'm sure she had me pegged as some kind of yoga stalker.

About three-quarters of the way through the class, I came to the strange realization that I was sweating, and not just a little but a lot! I wasn't quite to human river stage but I could feel the perspiration rolling down my back and soaking into the waistband of my underwear. This made no sense at all. I wasn't lifting weights or biking. I was—and there is no other way to describe it—moving slowly. Very slowly. Slowly extending my arms. Slowly extending my legs. Slowly rocking back and forth. This was not exercise. It was more like giving yourself a massage—that same relaxed feeling, that same release of tension.

The class ended the way it began, with us all lying on our backs with our eyes closed. Instead of the poem, though, the instructor brought out a guitar and sang to us. It was nice until I went to get up and the room began to spin. I suffer from a bit of vertigo. I've been afflicted with this most of my adult life. It's rarely a problem unless I get up from a reclining position too fast; then I get horribly dizzy and my stomach rises to my throat. It feels like I've just finished off a quart of gin but without any of the upside.

Despite the sweating and the reeling, I was back at yoga a week later, once again without Sylvia who had come up with a new and more inventive excuse: "I have to wash my hair."

As it did the previous week, the class started with a poem. As we lay on our backs, the instructor gently urged us to "become one with the earth below" and to "let our spirit take root." I had a hard time with this. Maybe I'm too literal, but the fact is that between the earth and me stood a slab of concrete and two floors of an underground parking garage. There was at least 30 feet of building and air between the earth and me, making it impossible for me to become one with it.

I was much better at yoga the second time. My movements were smoother and it became easier for me to follow what the instructor was asking us to do. But then it happened again. As I got up at the end of class, the room went into a drunken spin, achieving a level of nausea that took several hours to recover from.

Yoga was making me sick! This was not good. I made an appointment with my doctor. He did a full examination and found nothing wrong. I advocated for an MRI or a CAT scan or any other expensive tests he might have. My doctor claimed this would not be necessary. Instead, he suggested avoiding things that made me dizzy. I decided to heed his advice. Yoga is out as a possible retirement activity. I'm going to try meditation next. This, too, seems to work for my cat.

She can sit in the same position for hours staring at nothing and seems perfectly content. Maybe there is something to meditation.

Lloyd Bridges has got nothing on me!

Among my earliest memories is one of lying on the living room floor of my parents' house in my Flintstones pajamas watching Sea Hunt. It was the only show on TV that my parents allowed me to stay up past eight o'clock to see. No doubt this was a privilege won through a lot of intensive whining, but it was worth the effort. Sea Hunt was cool. Very cool. Lloyd Bridges was my hero.

Back then, lots of shows on TV featured a good guy who overcame a bad guy (in fact, every one of them did), but Lloyd was different. He did it underwater. Each week he would overcome countless dangers—all while being 50, 60, 70 or even 100 feet below the ocean's surface. I loved every minute of it. I squirmed when Lloyd was chased by sharks, which happened with surprising frequency. I said the prayers of a 6-year-old when he was trapped by an underwater cave collapse with no seeming way to free himself as the air in his tanks slowly ran out. And if all of that wasn't enough excitement, you could always count on a few episodes in which some ne'er-do-well with a spear gun would try to turn Lloyd into 180 pounds of prime fish food. Luckily, Lloyd never failed to cut the other guy's air hose first, thereby rendering him incapable of continuing the fight.

Lloyd faced so many dangers that if he were any normal person, he would have avoided the water altogether. But not Lloyd. He was brave and he proved his courage every week.

At age 6, I didn't think television could get any better. I was wrong. First came the invention of color TV, a miracle in itself. Next came Jacques Cousteau and his legendary ship, the Calypso. In my opinion, Jacques single-handedly made the invention of color TV worthwhile—at least for the lucky few who had one. Owing to my mother and father's incredible frugality, we were the last home on the planet to get a color TV. Indulge me while I present this sad but true story from my childhood: My parents waited until I left for college before buying a color TV. To this day, I believe they held off so long as payback for my decade of whining over their refusal to replace our pitiful black and white television. As I often explained to my parents and will share here, the only reason I survived my childhood was because my best friend Rob had parents who loved their children enough to go out and buy a color TV. It didn't matter that the screen was only 19 inches. It didn't matter that the picture was fuzzy. It didn't matter that if you even looked at the rabbit ears wrong, let alone touch them, the cathode ray tube would die a slow death, starting with wavy lines at the top and bottom of the screen and ending in a cataclysmic blizzard of snow. Whatever the limitations of 1960s technology or of my parents' affections, the fact remained: Jacques Cousteau was awesome. He transported us into the colorful world of tropical fish and beautiful coral. It was like nothing I'd ever seen, and I had watched every Sea Hunt episode at least twice.

Needless to say, I wanted to experience this fantastic world firsthand. When I was about 10, after what probably involved a lot of intensive yet-in-this-case-successful whining, my parents agreed to take the family camping to the nearest shore for a week—Rehoboth Beach, Delaware. I was ready. I had my plastic fins, my plastic facemask, my plastic snorkel and my plastic shark knife, which could only have actually killed a shark if it somehow got lodged in the beast's throat while he was slowly eating me. I practiced with them every night in the bathtub for a month in preparation for the big trip. I may not have had everything I needed to go Scuba diving, but I could picture myself lying on the surface watching the fish frolicking below. This was going to be the single greatest experience of my life and possibly the greatest experience that any 10-year-old has ever had, anytime, anywhere.

The reality turned out to be a far cry from what I had imagined. The beach was fun but it was not the Jacques Cousteau or Lloyd Bridges experience I yearned for. I realized this right away when I walked into water six or seven inches deep and immediately lost sight of my feet. My first thought was "God-

Damn-Jesus-Christ-Son-of-a-Bitch (see chapter on woodworking), what kind of ocean is this?" By the time I ventured far enough to be waist deep, I began to imagine all the villainous sea creatures that Lloyd had encountered on his adventures. The difference was that he could at least see them. I couldn't see my hand if I put it just inches below the surface. Most of my body had disappeared beneath the cold, murky waters of the breaking surf. I began to worry about the safety of my extremities: my feet, my hands and my private parts, especially my private parts. At the time, I had no idea of how these parts were to be used, but I did have some sense that they had a higher purpose than just hanging awkwardly between my legs. I was worried and rightly so. For all I knew, a hoard of hungry sharks could have been circling me right then and there and I wouldn't have a clue of this until one of the sharp-tooth bastards dragged me underwater, never to be seen again. Gone would be me, private parts and all.

As I grew older, I learned to love the Delaware shore, and my private parts, for what they did have to offer. This is particularly true when I became old enough to appreciate the sight of young women in tiny bikinis. That alone was worth the three-hour drive from home. In fact, at 16, seeing Diane Sloan, a high school classmate, in her swimsuit was a memory I would have crawled on my hands and knees across broken glass and burning coals in a month-long quest to get to the beach just to have experienced. She was that pretty. I got to talk to her for a good five minutes while she stood in front of me in a white bikini that covered a perfect, tightly packaged body wrapped in a radiant golden tan. I have no idea what she said. I have no idea what I said, other than knowing it apparently wasn't interesting enough to hold her attention for more than five minutes. But to this day I have total recall for the way she looked on that fine summer afternoon. Thanks to Diane and countless other young ladies who liked to spend their summers worshiping the sun at the beach, I came to appreciate that the Delaware shore had a lot going for it. The shore became the weekend destination for hundreds high school kids who would overrun the state campground at Cape Henlopen. Countless good times. For all its charm, though, the ocean at the Delaware shore was not the Caribbean (think jellyfish and horseshoe crabs rather than clownfish and lobsters), and my dreams of Lloyd Bridges and Jacques Cousteau were put on hold.

Eventually I met and married Sylvia, a wonderful woman who likes to travel as much as I do and who, by the way, is 10 times hotter than Diane Sloan ever was even on her best day. Our first trip together was to Hawaii, where we went snorkeling in beautiful, clear blue water. It was fantastic! I had finally found it—my Cousteau world. Just off the beach were hundreds of vibrant fish darting in and out of the coral heads in water so clear you felt you could see all the way to China. Tiny blue iridescent fish fought with orange and white clownfish while rays of sunlight danced off the ocean floor. I was hooked.

Our next vacation took us to the Virgin Islands, where I experienced my first resort course dive. For those who are not sure if they want to commit to the time and expense it takes to get dive-certified, a resort course offers a way to literally test the waters. For about $100 (maybe more these days), an instructor will take you into a pool to go over the basics and then for a shallow dive. Diving isn't for everyone. Some people can't get used to the equipment or the idea of wearing 14 pounds of weights and dropping off the side of a boat. Others have a tough time equalizing the pressure as they go deeper underwater. I experienced none of that. I loved it. I took to diving like a fish to water. To my surprise, I found that Scuba diving is easier than snorkeling. Once you drop a few feet, you no longer have to deal with the wave action at the surface.

I became dive certified 25 years ago in the small town of Guanica in southwestern Puerto Rico. My dive instructor, Max, was every bit of 75 years old. He had pure white hair and skin so dark and leather-like it was hard to tell his ethnicity. I took an immediate liking to him. This was a guy who clearly enjoyed what he was doing, and why not? He was living in paradise, in a dive town where being a little crazy was a requirement of residency. Max seemed to fit in perfectly. My first indication that he might be a little eccentric was when he explained that he was a retired veteran of both the U.S. and Canadian navies, although he was rather vague as to how that came to be. Having heard his story over a few beers, I'm not sure to this day whether he had really lived two lives or whether he had perhaps killed someone in a bar fight and assumed the guy's identity for the purposes of cashing an extra retirement check. Later, Max confirmed his unique view on life by describing in detail his favorite way to dive, which was to throw a lounge chair over the side of the boat, take it to the bottom, set it up near a coral head and wait for the fish to come to him. I have no doubt that if Max had figured out how to drink beer while submerged, a six-pack would have accompanied him on every dive. His enthusiasm for everything he did made me jealous. Max had a zest for life and he was a great role model for retirement.

Diving is the closest most of us will ever come to being on another planet. It is other-worldly. I've swum with more sea turtles that I can count. These are beautiful creatures who take life slow and live a very long time—a lesson for all of us. I've followed lobsters as they've marched across the sand between coral heads and marveled at just how ugly and awkward they are. Once I was surprised by a large green moray eel jealously guarding its home who seemed concerned that I might be interested in moving in. I assured him I was already saddled to a mortgage I couldn't afford and we both moved on. Lesson learned. I've seen countless species of fish, including more than a few sharks, none of which seemed to have even the remotest interest in eating me. I am, of course, grateful but also slightly miffed that I might not look appealing enough to serve as a dinner entree. Off the coast of one Caribbean island, I swam for a good 10 minutes with a family of cuttlefish that clearly had no interest in cuddling and would turn bright red whenever I got too close. In the waters of the Galapagos, I watched in awe as a family of penguins dove with incredible speed through a school of sardines, dining on whatever they could catch.

In the years since becoming certified, I've been on at least 50 dives. Unfortunately, my last dive was 5 years ago. I've just been too busy to fit it in. But this is a hobby I will definitely get back to. Sylvia and I have already planned a trip to Guadeloupe.

I owe a debt of gratitude to my hero, Lloyd Bridges, and to Jacques Cousteau for turning me on to this incredible pastime.

Board games
as blood sport

I have a confession to make. Over the past 12 years, I've played an estimated 6,000 online games of Backgammon while at work. Here's the math: two games a day (I probably averaged more) for at least 12 years equals 5,760 games. Other than eating and going to the bathroom, I can't think of anything else I've done more than 5,760 times.

If you figure five minutes per game, that comes to 480 hours or about 12 weeks of my career that I spent playing the game. That's like getting an extra week of paid vacation in each of the last dozen years.

I was shocked when I added it up. Not nearly as shocked, though, as a lawyer friend who reviewed an early draft of this chapter prior to publication. Her exact words: "Are you fucking nuts?" In less colorful language she went on to explain that, since I was still working and not yet officially retired, I could easily be fired for admitting this level of goofing off. She wanted me to kill the chapter. Instead, we settled on a compromise in which I agreed to include the following disclaimer:

This chapter has been highly exaggerated for comedic value. As an ethical person, I would never, ever steal from my employer. This includes but is not limited to physical items, such as the many, many reams of paper that seemed to disappear from the supply closet in recent months. None of these have been surreptitiously taken night after night, secured in a not-so-secret compartment in my briefcase, and none of those sheets of paper were used to print out the countless early drafts of this book. I also am not responsible for the disappearance of a case of extra-large Post-it Notes (don't you just LOVE Post-it Notes!) or any of the Precise "Fine Point" Roller Ball Pens which are the best pens ever made and that retail for nearly $6.00 each at Office Max. (Hey, when you're facing a future on a fixed income, every dollar counts!) And while Betty the security guard may have suspected otherwise, there have been no boxes of these fine pens stuffed down my pants as I've left the building each night. I really was just happy to see her.

In addition to physical items, this also includes any perceived theft by actions I may or may not have engaged in at work such as playing an excessive number of online games while "on the clock." I furthermore would never try to justify these actions by pointing out that for 30 years, I willingly sat through the monthly two-hour staff meetings, clapping wholeheartedly for every new intern who was introduced, even though I really didn't care who the new crop of interns were or where they came from or what college they were attending, and even though I secretly resented each and every one of them for their youth and unbridled enthusiasm.

Frankly, I didn't think a disclaimer was necessary since most games were played at my desk while I ate lunch, but I figure my attorney knows what she is talking about.

Now that we've established that this entire chapter is complete fiction, let's move on.

After nearly 6,000 online games of Backgammon, I reached two conclusions:

- I must really like this game.
- I must be incredibly good at it. After all, no one plays the same game 6,000 times without getting good at it, right?

I began to wonder what it would be like to play against real people—the flesh-and-blood kind and not the anonymous, digitized online versions people present on the web. This would be fun on two levels. First, I would get to meet new people who share an interest in a game I really like. Second, I would get to use my vast skills acquired through 6,000+ games to defeat all of them, savoring each victory to satisfy my inherent need to prove to myself and to the world that I am the top dog: the alpha male.

This last point is important. Almost every job comes with a certain amount of competition. If you are a salesman, for example, your success can be measured in sales totals. If you come out on top, you can take pride in knowing that in a head-to-head competition with your peers, you smoked their sorry asses. Victory is yours, with all the recognition, the glory and the personal satisfaction that comes with it, at least until next month's numbers come in. For a lot of people, myself included, competition provides a sense of self-worth and I fear losing this ego booster in retirement. My job, especially early in my career, was filled with competitive situations. But unlike high school, where this usually involved games with balls, these were adult competitions with bigger risks and rewards. I loved every minute of it and celebrated every victory. Over time, though, the nature of my job changed and the competitions disappeared, replaced by welcomed promotions accompanied by increasingly bureaucratic responsibilities. In some small way, Backgammon helped satisfy my competitive demons. In retirement, I figured, Backgammon could still fill this need. Playing against real people and seeing the agony of defeat on their faces as I crushed them could even take this up a notch. The problem was I had no idea how to connect with other people who liked to play Backgammon.

Often when faced with these kinds of perplexing problems, I turn to the only source of information I can really trust—the Internet. A quick Google search turned up a multi-state Backgammon tournament being held in just six weeks and only an hour from my house. It sounded great. Not only could I play against real people but I could beat them in a real tournament! This would be fun. I signed up immediately and mailed off my check.

A week later, Richard, the tournament coordinator, called me with a host of questions, like: "What level do you play?" "Are you participating in any of the side pools?" and "Would you like to join any of the blitzes, quickies or doubles?"

My responses went something like: "There are levels?" "What's a side pool? "Quickies and doubles? Are we still talking about Backgammon?"

Richard found no humor in this. He suggested that prior to the tournament I might want to test my skills by joining other players at any number of bars around town that have regularly scheduled Backgammon nights.

I loved that idea! I would be able to hone my skills in advance of the tournament by taking down some easy competition in a local bar. Could it get any better!

The following Monday night found me in a bar in Virginia meeting up with 20 other people who share an interest in Backgammon. For me, this was not as easy as it sounds. At heart, I am an introvert. I come from a long line of introverts. I have no doubt that my ancestors were not only cave dwellers but were of the hermit variety. I can picture them living alone at the bottom of some mountain (if they are anything like me, they would have been too lazy to live at the top); rarely venturing out except maybe to occasionally copulate before returning to a blissful life of solitude.

As inviting as it sounds, being an introvert is not all it is cracked up to be. At least work forced me into a community of people from varying backgrounds with (mostly) shared goals. I know I need to find something similar in retirement. Backgammon offers this opportunity.

Like any dice-based game, Backgammon involves a lot of luck. But it also requires a great deal of skill. The "luck" aspect of the game is minimized in competitive play by basing matches on multiple games with each game initially counting as a point. Most matches are won by the competitor who is the first to win five points. In high-dollar events, the bar can rise to as many as 25 points. Skill comes into play on two levels. First, a skillful player must know how to make the most of whatever roll of the dice he or she gets. Second, a competitor must know when (and whether) to double the stakes.

For the bar competition, each player put $20 into a pot. The overall winner of the night would get half the money, with second and third place finishers splitting the rest. So, I had a chance of winning $200 for the evening.

For my first match, I was teamed up against Evan. The game started out well but as it progressed, Evan was clearly taking a lead. About a third of the way in, he moved to double the stakes. I knew my best play would be to forfeit, but it was the first game of my first match and I wanted to play it through. I accepted the double. Things went quickly downhill after that. Evan not only won but managed to get all his pieces off the board before I could remove any of mine. This is called a gammon. Evan won the two points, plus an additional double because of the gammon, for a total of four points in one game. It did not look good for me. I clawed my way back, winning the next three games, but Evan won an additional game for a total of five points and the match.

My second match of the evening was for three points. My opponent and I traded games until I finally lost three to two. Two losses meant I was out of the competition for the night and on my way home. My opponent was gracious in victory, suggesting a book I might want to read.

I bought the book online and spent much of the following week reading its incomprehensible advice. It might as well have been written in a completely foreign language. Something must have rubbed off, however, because a week later I was back in the bar and won my first three games in a row. As the fourth game started, my opponent looked worried. He was taking a little more time with each move. At one point, I watched as his eyes darted across the board, from piece to piece, first his, then mine. It took me a minute to realize that what he was doing was counting the total number of spaces every piece would have to move to secure a victory for either side. With the help of a pad of paper, an adding machine and a lot of time, I could have done the same calculations, but he was doing it in his head and in less than a minute. I lost the next two games, making the score three to two. I rallied to take my fourth game, just one shy of victory, but it wasn't to happen. My opponent won the next three games in a row, taking the match five to four.

My next opponent not only beat me in straight sets but did it in record time. I was out of competition for the rest of the night. He annihilated me so quickly that he had a lot of time to kill while waiting for his next competitor. I invited him to join me at the bar for a beer.

"You know about this club, right?" he asked as we waited for the bartender.

"What do you mean?"

"These guys .... You know who you're playing against?"

Up to this point, I figured I had been playing against some smart guys who really liked Backgammon. But the way he asked the question made me realize there might be more to it. "Maybe not," I replied.

"That first guy you played tonight, he consistently ranks in the top 10 in the country. See the guy he's playing against now? He just got back from a tournament in Georgia, and I don't mean the state. I mean the country. He won a lot of money."

Then he pointed to a guy I had played against the week before.

"He was in Vegas not long ago and came in seventh in the national championships. You shouldn't feel bad about losing to anybody here. This club has some of the best players in the world."

I not only didn't feel bad, I felt considerably better. Maybe I hadn't won a single match, but I had won quite a few games against some of the best players anywhere. I was feeling good.

That would quickly change.

The bartender brought over the beers and I picked up the tab.

"Your game's not too bad," my opponent continued, "but you really have to figure out when to double. You suck at that. More games are won by knowing how to play the doubling cube than knowing how to move the checkers."

"Well, I have two weeks to get better," I said. "I'm playing in the tournament at the end of the month."

"What level did you sign up for?" he asked.

"Intermediate."

"That's no good," he offered. "The tournament attracts the best players on the East Coast. You play intermediate and you'll be out in the first 15 minutes. You would be better off signing up for the novice group."

While I wondered if I should feel a little insulted by the suggestion I play against novices, my opponent continued with his advice.

"You should pick up some books, too."

I mentioned the one I bought.

"No. No. No. That's for serious players. You should pick up *Backgammon for Dummies*. It's a good starting point for beginners."

I always feel insulted by the Dummies books. Buying them seems like an admission of stupidity. I expect books like *Cooking for Dummies* to begin with a chapter about turning on the stove followed by helpful hints on proper methods for opening and closing a refrigerator. Yet there was no way *Backgammon for Dummies* could be worse than the first book I read, so I decided to take his advice. I bought the book. It turned out to be surprisingly helpful. I also signed up for novice group in the tournament.

Two weeks later I found myself at a Holiday Inn out by the airport with well over a hundred competitors. Most were in the intermediate or advanced classes. I would be playing four others in the novice class, all of whom had experience in tournament play.

The first things that caught my eye were the competitors' boards. Each was a work of art, with fine inlaid woods inside buttery leather cases. If someone had told me their checkers were made of solid gold, I would not have been the slightest bit surprised. I slid my $28 board from K-Mart over to a corner of the room and pretended it wasn't mine.

My first match was against a young man who played every week at a local club. He seemed like a very nice person until the moment I beat him. He was not happy about the loss. I could tell this because at the end of the final game, he pushed back from the table and accused me of winning only because I'd had "lucky rolls." This, I was to learn later, is a hard-hitting insult in the world of Backgammon, the equivalent of being called a "no-skill hack." In the expert class, this level of insult might result in a serious verbal exchange and some wounded feelings. In my case, though, I had to admit the guy had a point. I had won mostly because of some really lucky rolls.

My second match was against a sweet, elderly woman who approached each game as though it were blood sport. After every move I made, she would slowly shake her head back and forth and mumble something in a heavy eastern European accent, as if to say, "That was such a bad move" or "I don't think this one's ready for the novice class," or "Shame, shame ... and he was so close to winning." I quickly realized that this was her way of trying to psych me out. When she saw it wasn't going to work, she stopped doing it and we started having a really good time. She was lively and fun. Unfortunately for her, my luck with the dice held throughout the match and I beat her in all but two games.

My luck continued to hold for the third and fourth matches. There was hardly an open blot I couldn't hit, a critical point I couldn't make or a double I couldn't roll. If there is any truth to beginner's luck, I had it that night. After seven straight hours of play, and four matches totaling 33 games (22 of which I won), I emerged as the only player in our small group to be undefeated. This made me the overall winner of the novice category. My nearly 6,000 games of online Backgammon had paid off. I was victorious. I was the alpha male. Maybe it was just the novice class but I was happy to bask in the glory and to accept my plaque and the $163 in prize money.*

I was feeling good!

It wouldn't last.

I got up early the next morning and dropped in on a lecture for the serious players on Backgammon strategy. I looked at the group gathered around the presenter, who had flown in from Japan. They all seemed to have something in common. At first, I couldn't make it out. Then it occurred to me: Have you ever wondered what happened to all the nerds you went to high school with? I'm not talking about the kids in the Audio Visual Club. I know what happened to them; I was in the AV club myself. I'm talking about the kids in the math or chemistry clubs, the kids who were so smart they seemed to have their own language, the kids who went on to schools like MIT and Carnegie Mellon. I realized I was sitting in a room with them all. It felt like I had accidentally stumbled into a Mensa meeting where I clearly didn't belong. I watched in amazement as the presenter set up a scenario on the board and then asked questions like: "If white rolls a six and a three, what is his best move?" The serious players would then engage in a strong debate around the question, throwing out observations like, "If he makes that move, white's odds of winning drop from 37% to 23%." Then someone would chime in with a comment like, "You're wrong; it doesn't drop to 23%, it drops to 26%." Each scenario would elicit heated arguments until someone broke out a computer, set up the scenario and verify the correct percentage. I realized that guys playing at this level could take one look at a board and calculate the odds of winning in their heads. It was humbling and more than a little scary.

I will never be that good. Ever.

I walked out of the lecture thinking that what I need is a Backgammon club full of novices. Or perhaps take up competitive checkers.

NOTE: If anyone affiliated with the IRS is reading this, let me remind you of the above disclaimer stating that everything in this chapter has been exaggerated for comedic effect. This includes the amount of the prize money.

Breathing good, drowning bad

I like breathing. I've been doing it my entire life. Breathing is the very first thing I learned to do, and over the years I've gotten very good at it. My secret? I practice. I practice a lot, every day, all day. 24-7-365-60+. All that practice has paid off. I've reached the point where I don't even have to think about breathing when I am doing it. I can take deep breaths. I can take shallow breaths. I can take every kind of breath in between. I can even breathe in my sleep.

What I'm *not* good at is *not* breathing. In fact, I am bad, very bad, at not breathing, but I'm getting ahead of the story …

For more than 30 years, Sylvia and I have lived in Washington, D.C., less than a mile from the Potomac River, in one of the best whitewater kayaking areas on the East Coast. Our part of the city is home to a large cult of kayakers. By day, these people work as lawyers, accountants and lobbyists, but on evenings and weekends they transform into some sort of aging kayak version of Moon Doggie and Gidget. These are people like our close neighbor who drives around all winter with a kayak strapped to the top of his car "just in case the weather changes." They are obsessed. I've seen 90-year-old cult members with walkers negotiating the trail to the river's edge while dragging their kayak behind them. Okay, that was a bit of an exaggeration, but I have stood on the edge of a cliff and watched kayakers go over Great Falls, which is one small step less crazy than going over Niagara Falls in a kayak.

Yet, to hear them talk, it's all great fun. So we decided to try it.

We signed up for the first of a recommended four whitewater kayaking classes. I imagined myself paddling down the river like the early Indians. I expected to learn how to navigate some fun, but not death-defying, beginner rapids and was looking forward to the chance to meet other soon-to-be cult members. This was going to be a great day.

It wasn't. It was horrible. Not horrible like finding out your dog just died; more like taking a vacation to a Caribbean island only to have it rain the entire week. That kind of horrible.

To begin with, we never made it to the river. The entire five-hour class was conducted in the waters of the 150-year-old C&O Canal that runs parallel to the river. The canal looks nothing like the majestic Potomac River; more like an aging open intake pipe to a water treatment facility. It smelled only marginally better. Instead of learning to paddle or navigate rapids, the class focused solely on one thing: what to do if you find yourself upside down in your kayak. According to Arnie, the instructor, this happens a lot. As he tells it, whitewater kayakers often find themselves with the keel of the boat facing the sky while their faces are dragged along the river bottom as they frantically work to avoid colliding head on into giant underwater boulders. Arnie further pointed out that even if you do manage to avoid the rocks, you still will drown unless you know how to right the kayak.

Arnie had my attention.

Drowning is not on my list of preferred ways to die (number one is to go out like Nelson Rockefeller*).

We began on land with a simple exercise to see how long we could each hold our breath. Ten seconds into this, my body came to life demanding to know just what I was doing. It wasn't so much that I needed oxygen right away. The problem was that my body wanted to know why, after so many uninterrupted years of continuous breathing, I had suddenly stopped. It urged me to begin again immediately lest we forget how and risk being unable to resume. At 20 seconds, my body was beginning to feel a legitimate need for oxygen and strongly questioned why I was actively suppressing its attempts to get some. At 30 seconds, panic began spreading through my body faster than an arson fire in a textile mill. At 40 seconds, I threw in the towel. I was not alone.

While not fun, the exercise did teach one valuable life lesson—I really don't like holding my breath. Unfortunately, there was much more of this to come.

Lesson two involved getting comfortable with the idea of being upside down in a kayak. I was not keen on doing this. I'll concede that maybe I should have paid more attention to the course description and its references to "learning the basics," but nowhere did it clearly define the basics. Besides, it was too late to back out. If there is one thing I learned in junior high school, it's that you never want to come off looking like the class wimp. So I willingly sat in my kayak in the middle of the canal while Arnie tipped it over. Right away, I discovered it was far easier to hold my breath under water than on dry land. I think it had to do with the knowledge that if I tried to breathe, gallons of murky water would immediately cascade deep into my lungs and, if this didn't immediately kill me, would undoubtedly cause some kind of bacterial infection immune to all known antibiotics and result in a slow and painful death. Proper motivation, I learned, was clearly key to holding my breath longer than 40 seconds. Eventually, Arnie righted the craft. Arnie was my hero, at least until he tipped me over again. Arnie did this several times. He seemed to be enjoying himself.

The next lesson focused on how to signal for help while upside down in a kayak. This involved tipping over the kayak, then reaching up above the water line and banging frantically on the sides of the boat in hopes that another kayaker, or possibly a family of specially trained rescue beavers (Arnie told us all about them), would come to save you. The whole time I was underwater all I could think of was, "What if no one comes?" What if all the other kayakers are,

74

like me, upside down in their boats frantically banging away hoping for someone to rescue them? And what of these rescue beavers? What is their track record of success? What kind of training do they go through? Do they have proper certification? Do they know CPR? Mouth-to-mouth resuscitation? Then it occurred to me, "Good God, what if they are on vacation?" And that was the image that stuck in my head as I flailed around upside down, wildly banging on the sides of the kayak —the vision of a family of beavers, my rescue beavers, lounging poolside at some resort drinking fancy umbrella drinks while I drowned in a smelly canal without ever having actually kayaked on the Potomac River.

Just shy of giving up all hope of rescue, I felt my fingers being crushed between the side of my kayak and the bow of another person's boat. I clutched at the bow like a drowning man offered a life line (which I nearly was) and pulled myself up with enough force that I was sure to sink the other boat. The sight of blue sky was wonderful. As I looked around, however, I couldn't help but notice that there were no beavers in sight.

Lesson learned: During August in Washington, everyone is on vacation, including the rescue beavers.

Sensing my anxiety, Arnie suggested that one way to feel calmer underwater and avoid panicking would be to imagine myself in my "happy place." So the next time Arnie tipped over my kayak, I tried very hard to find my happy place. Unfortunately, my happy place turned out to be an image of myself sitting upright in a kayak staring at blue sky and taking full, deep breaths. Every time Arnie rolled my kayak, my brain would do all it could to force my body to take whatever action necessary to get to that happy place AS QUICKLY AS POSSIBLE.

You can, we learned, right a kayak all on your own. This involves a complex set of maneuvers that require correctly positioning your paddle while quickly thrusting your hip against the side of the boat. Done right, you pop back up to the surface like a cork. Arnie made it look easy. Arnie was a bit of a show-off. However, in practicing this complicated water dance, I discovered that the hip thrust involves using a set of muscles that either I don't have or which have completely atrophied. On the third attempt, my body expressed its opposition by producing a grapefruit-sized Charlie horse deep in the right rear of my gluteus maximus. On land, this would not have been a big problem. A 10- to 15-foot walk would have worked out most of the pain. But I wasn't on land. I was wedged into a kayak that had less room to maneuver than the average coffin. It hurt. A gunshot to the ass would have been less painful. Sitting on a smoldering campfire would have been a welcome relief because at least then I could have bent my knees. The only comfort I could take, while the pain marched north to my shoulders and south to the tips of my toes, was in knowing that the class would soon end. Surely it had to end!

And that brings us to the last lesson of the day. Arnie explained that when all else fails, a kayaker can quickly exit the craft by pulling the cord that releases the skirt used to seal a person into the boat. We practiced this several times. It was simple. I was good at it. I can honestly say that no one in the class could get out of an upside-down kayak as quickly as I could. No one. In fact, I may hold the world record at this.

The exercise led me to ask Arnie the obvious question: "Why is this the last option and not the first?" Arnie smiled, giving me some indication that I was not the first to ask this question. "Because once you are out of the kayak, you are swimming and you are no longer kayaking." I understood his point but you also are not drowning.

By the time the class ended, I was ready to give up my dream of kayaking. There would be no initiation into the cult, no hazing and no secret handshake. With much disappointment, I began to stow my gear. But then I noticed another class of students who appeared at the launch point. Their kayaks looked different, a little larger and wider. Arnie explained that these were flat-water kayaks designed to be much more stable than whitewater kayaks. He said they were almost impossible to roll.

Again, Arnie had my attention.

A week later, Sylvia and I were back on the river with a class of flat-water kayakers. It was great.

After a few basic lessons, none of which involved holding my breath or struggling upside down in the river, we spent most of the day gently paddling up the C&O Canal, then portaged over a bit of land and paddled down the Potomac River. It was amazing to be a few miles from a major city while floating down a river watching blue herons along the banks while bald eagles circled overhead. The best part of the trip was crossing the Potomac below Seneca Flats.

There was just enough current to make the trip challenging but nothing close to death defying and with virtually no risk of tipping over. It was a lot of fun.

The instructor warned us to keep a sharp eye out for more interesting wildlife—a middle-aged couple who liked to kayak out to the rocks midway between the shores and sunbathe in the nude. Frankly, it didn't sound like a bad way to spend the day. Sadly, though, we had no sightings of this elusive wildlife.

Our class had nine students ranging in age from 20-something to at least three of us who were 60-plus. The instructor was probably the oldest of all of us and was clearly someone who had found his life's passion at an early age and had never stopped doing it.

Overall, Sylvia and I decided that flat-water kayaking was more our speed. I'll probably never keep a kayak strapped to the roof of my car but I'm sure this will stay in my retirement portfolio.

Nelson Rockefeller, former governor of New York and vice president of the United States, died of a massive heart attack while in bed with his 25-year-old, very attractive blonde "assistant." All things considered, there are far worse ways to go. I've discussed my death preference with Sylvia. She is okay with me going out like Nelson but only if she passes away first. This seems reasonable to me.

Wood, smoke, beer
and the basement

Everyone has certain smells that trigger memories of childhood. For some, it's fresh baked cookies. For others, it's the scent of their mother's perfume or the pleasing odor of a simple peanut butter and jelly sandwich. For me it's the aroma of freshly cut wood mixed with voluminous clouds of cigarette smoke. That was the smell of my home as a child. That was the smell of my father.

Woodworking was my dad's hobby and he loved it. He would disappear into the basement for a few hours every evening after dinner to work on projects. The rest of us would sit in the living room watching TV while the sounds of the circular saw, the drill press and other power tools vibrated through the house. To a 3- or 4-year-old, these were scary sounds. Every so often the basement would go strangely quiet and then we'd hear my dad suddenly yell, "God-Damn-Jesus-Christ-Son-of-a-Bitch," said so quickly that it sounded like a single nine-syllable word. Being young, I was, of course, a sponge when it came to things like that and, much to my mother's consternation, by age 6, I could curse better than most sailors and certainly better than anyone else in first grade. This was perhaps the first useful lesson I learned from my father and one I've put into practice every day since.

The basement was my father's domain, a place for men, a place where young children were not allowed. It was a place where he could express his creativity and where he could escape for a bit of time alone. Every so often he would carry up some sort of piece of furniture and present it to Mom as proof that his time was well spent. Then he would disappear back into the basement.

Eventually I reached an age when my dad stopped disappearing alone into the basement and began to invite me along. I was thrilled. I was his apprentice. I held the lumber. I fetched the tools. I ran upstairs to get him a beer and usually another one or two after that. It was great.

Together, we tackled all kinds of projects, and not just woodworking. Rooms were painted. A porch was constructed off the back of the house. Next came a garden shed complete with a cement pad for the floor —25 cubic feet of cement mixed by hand (I suspect he did most of the work). We even built a canoe. It weighed about a hundred times more than an aluminum canoe and required a team of 27 dedicated volunteers to get it onto the car's roof rack, but we could proudly point to the product of our work. Lots of people had store-bought canoes. We built ours by hand, just like the Indians, except that we used a power saw, drill, and lots and lots of clamps.

When I was about 11, my dad decided to grow orchids. I have no idea where he came up with such an idea. Up to that point I can't remember him ever watering a plant, including the yard. But the next day found us building the only greenhouse within 25 miles of our home. Half the people in the neighborhood didn't know what it was. The other half probably thought it was for growing pot.

At some point Dad and I went through a clock phase, constructing carriage clocks, steeple clocks, Eli Terry clocks and even a grandfather clock, all with fine wooden cases of black walnut (his favorite wood) or cherry or maple. Finally, we had to stop. The sound of so many clocks in the house, all ticking away and chiming every 15 minutes, made it nearly impossible to sleep. It was downright torture if you had even a mild case of insomnia. Building these clocks, though, was my first real introduction to the symmetry of classic forms and the beginning of my appreciation of good design.

We did it all. We did it together. We did it by ourselves. Dad was not the kind of guy who saw the world in black and white, far from it. He did have one unshakable rule, though—you never, never, ever, ever, ever, ever, ever, under any circumstances, any at all, paid someone to do work you could do yourself. This applied to carpentry, plumbing, electrical work, roofing, painting, auto repair or anything else. If my mom had let him, he would have applied this rule to dentistry, resetting bone fractures, orthodontics and minor surgery. Central to this philosophy was a fundamental belief that it didn't matter whether you knew how to do something because if you applied yourself, you could always "god-damn-well" figure it out. Time and time again we proved this to be true. Whatever we tackled always turned out well, with one exception—a plumbing job that some say was completely my fault. In my defense, however, who puts a blowtorch in the hands of a 12-year-old? I mean really, no good can come from that.

When I look back on my childhood with the benefit of hindsight, it amazes me that we tackled so many different projects. This is particularly true because I have no idea how my dad knew how to do these things. He never really had a father he could rely on or learn from, at least not one he ever talked about. I have a vague memory of being 4 or 5 years old and listening as the adults talked about my grandfather's recent death. It was, to the best of my recollection, the one and only time he was ever mentioned in our home. My father's upbringing was so shrouded in mystery that I later became convinced our family was in the witness protection program. To this day, I'm not sure we weren't. I've often wondered what crime he may have committed or what horrible atrocity he may have witnessed. Watching gangster movies, I've tried to imagine my dad in the role of the tough guy, but it never seems to fit. He was too decent.

But I digress ...

As I grew older, hanging out with my friends became far more important to me than hanging out with my dad. But he kept going, moving from clocks to turning bowls on a lathe. These were beautiful creations of curly maple and burl walnut. He kept making bowls well into his 80s, until his eyes gave out.

My dad died in 2012. A few years later, we persuaded my mom to move into a retirement community (see chapter: "A shoe bag future"). It was while cleaning out the basement in preparation for selling the house that I came across two slabs of black walnut. Each was about six feet long. One was 18 inches wide and the other 16. This was not the kind of lumber you get at Home Depot. These were rough-cut planks, each at least an inch and a half thick, with bark remaining on the edges. I took one look at them and decided to build something I would use every day that would remind me of my dad. I would build a desk.

Great ideas sometimes get put on hold because of the demands of the moment. The wood went into my basement to sit for a few years until I had the time and a vision of what I wanted to build. Then a few months ago I came across two beautiful decorative cast iron grates at a flea market. I realized that with some clever woodworking they would be perfect for the legs of the desk.

The project was on!

The starting point of a project with my dad was always a trip to the lumberyard. This is where real men gathered on Saturday mornings—big men with flannel shirts and blue jeans, all smoking cigarettes while they waited by their trucks to pick up their loads. We couldn't afford a truck. Whatever we bought—two-by-fours, plywood, sheet rock, etc.—ended up on the roof of the car sitting on a set of old wooden racks held in place with suction cups and nylon straps that secured (although that might be too generous a word) them to the car's rain gutters. The ride home was always a gamble as to whether the payload would become airborne on its own or lift the car into the sky. Every curve was executed with great care lest the load continue its forward momentum while the car rounded the bend and headed in an entirely different direction.

Times have changed, and not necessarily for the better.

I started the desk project by calling around to see which lumber stores stocked walnut I could use for the table legs. None did. A Google search came up with close to 40 online stores happy to ship whatever walnut customers wanted. I'm no stranger to ordering online. In fact, I hate going into brick-and-mortar stores almost as much as I hate visiting the dentist. I buy everything I can online. Electronics. Groceries. Shoes. Even socks and underwear (not kidding). But ordering lumber online seemed weird. Despite misgivings, I gave in to the modern age and ordered on the web. Two days later the wood was delivered. I still felt cheated out of a trip to the lumberyard.

The first challenge was to build the desktop. I don't have the tools needed to plane the walnut, glue the pieces together and square them up. With no choice but to violate Dad's cardinal rule, I hired a company to do it. I cheated. But the rest of the job I did myself.

Over several days, with the table saw, radial arm saw, biscuit joiner and palm sander inherited from Dad, the desk began to take shape. I had forgotten how much fun it could be to work on a project where you saw immediate results. With each cut, I watched the desk coming together. I was amazed at what could be accomplished in a few hours. Here was something that didn't require a committee of 50 people, design and implementation teams, marketing experts or 87 planning and development meetings, each one lasting exactly the allotted time of one hour—no more, no less. Here was a project where the timeline was a week or two, not a two-year phase-in for a product guaranteed to be obsolete by the time it was completed.

God, it was good. But not without a few challenges. Amazingly, even though I had ganged all four legs together to cut them exactly the same length, one leg still came out longer than the others. This defied the basic laws of physics. It required me to stop what I was doing, stare at the four pieces for a minute and then let out my own "God-Damn-Jesus-Christ-Son-of-a-Bitch." Dad would have been proud. I felt much better. I understood at that moment the healing powers of my dad's basement mantra.

Assembling the table legs also reminded me of one of the points Dad used to make. It really helps to have the right tools. When it came time to glue the pieces together, I brought out my Dad's 50-year-old pipe clamps. I couldn't have done the job without them. Rarely do you come across something 50+ years old that is as useful today as when it was new. I take comfort in this.

The result of this effort is a beautiful desk I will use for years. Many of the later chapters in this book were written while sitting at it.

Is the job perfect? No. The legs are a little too high, owing to the size of the cast-iron grills. Overall, though, I really enjoyed this project and will be doing more woodworking. It's fun. It is a wonderful creative outlet. If there is a downside, it would be this—woodworking is not a social activity. When I was young, it was my dad and me. As I grew older, and particularly toward the end of his life, it was my dad alone in the basement and that's kind of sad to think about.

Those hours in the basement with him are among my fondest memories. The desk project brought them back to life. A lot of kids, including my dad, don't have someone willing to take the time to teach them anything of value. That is sad to think about as well, because what I really learned from the woodworking, carpentry, painting and plumbing we did together (aside from a few woodworking, carpentry, painting and plumbing skills) was never to be afraid of a project you didn't have the slightest idea how to do. I learned to view every challenge with enthusiasm and to have confidence that I could figure it out. And I learned that if, in the process, you happen to start a small fire with a blowtorch, well, that's okay, too. Whatever success I had in life I owe to these lessons my father taught me. I spent 12 years in public school, four years in college, two years at grad school, and none of it was as useful as this.

Floundering with fish

What I envy most about fish is that they get to live life completely free of the ground below them. We humans cannot say that. We can move forward and backward, right and left and even walk up and down, but almost all the time, unless assisted by mechanical devices or other contrivances, we remain bound to the earth below our feet. This is not the case for fish. They can swim higher or lower or just hover. They are free to roam with complete spatial freedom. Their only limitations are the surface above and the sea floor below. Everything in between is a world of endless options. They can dart around objects, swim over them or even, in some cases, under them. They have no need for highways or bridges, which is really good because there is not a fish anywhere smart enough to build one.

Which brings me to what I envy least about fish —they are stupid.

Over my 60+ years, I've met some dumb people. But I would venture to say that, with a couple of notable exceptions, even the dumbest among them is at least marginally smarter than the savviest of fish.

I feel I can speak with some authority about fish intelligence because I have a small pond in my yard filled with goldfish. I've studied them. They don't make or use tools. They don't build elaborate homes. They have no language skills. They seem incapable of remembering what happened as little as a minute ago, let alone yesterday. I suspect they spend little time contemplating the meaning of life or their own death.

To my surprise, however, they do seem to have a religious side. Every day I venture out to the pond with a heaping tablespoon of food. The fish gather at the surface with their heads poking out of the water and their mouths opening and closing with great anticipation. I have become, in their eyes, the Food God—giver of the nightly nutrition. I would like to explain to them that I am not a god, just a mere mortal crazy enough to build a fish pond, thus sentencing myself to a lifetime of cleaning the debris from the pond, making sure they are well fed and emptying the filter of their never-ending fish waste. But I can't because they are not smart enough to understand.

The weird part about fish intelligence is that they inhabited this planet long before we did. We evolved from them, or at least share a distant branch on the same family tree. Unlike them, however, we advanced on a steady path of evolutionary progress while they remained pretty much the same. There is little notable about their evolutionary path other than that singular moment when a brave fish ventured out of the water and onto land, taking one small step for fish and one giant leap for mankind.

My relationship with fish began when I was young and got my first plastic rod with magnetic fish that I could catch at the end of a string. I was hooked. By age 10, my best friend Rob and I spent our summers riding bikes from one fishing hole to another to see what we could catch. We fished Dupont's Pond, Lum's Pond, Steel's Pond, Red Clay Creek and as far as our bikes and our parents would let us. We lived a Tom Sawyer life, updated to the 1960s to include television and cars but devoid of today's helicopter parenting. As we got older, our range grew wider and even included, thanks to Rob's dad, a great trip to Lake George when we were about 14 to do some serious bass fishing.

Then it all seemed to stop, at least for me. I'm not sure exactly when I quit fishing or why. I liked fishing. I just stopped doing it. I think this may have coincided with reaching the age in which I discovered girls and decided to spend my time in what turned out to be a mostly (more accurate: completely) unsuccessful pursuit of them. Rob kept fishing though, and, to the best of my recollection, he also managed to reel in just about every young woman who came within 10 feet of him.

After high school our friendship faded but we reconnected at our 40th reunion. I think the bond among childhood friends is a little like that of a band of brothers in war, minus the bullets, of course, unless you happen to be growing up in Chicago. You go through so much together in those years from about 6 to 17 that you form a connection nearly impossible to replicate among adults and a depth of friendship which, despite years of little or no contact, is remarkably easy to rekindle.

So, when I decided to try fishing again, I called Rob.

His first question was, "What kind of fishing do you want to do?"

Truthfully, I hadn't given this any thought. As Rob ran through the options—from fly fishing to bass fishing and from freshwater to saltwater—I realized there are probably as many ways of fishing as there are species of fish. I confessed that I didn't know but was open to anything. He told me he would look into it and get back to me.

A couple of days later he called with a proposal. In a few weeks, he and his friend Greg were going to take Greg's boat 12 miles off the Delaware coast to fish for flounder. Was I in?

Somehow, in my mind, I was thinking about the old days of Beck's Pond and Dupont's Pond, Trap Pond and Lum's Pond, and all the other ponds. It hadn't occurred to me that in the 40+ intervening years, Rob's favorite fishing holes might have expanded to include the Atlantic Ocean. Frankly, I was a little concerned about this. The ocean is a very big pond and the sheer volume of water significantly increases the chances of drowning. You may recall from the chapter on kayaking that drowning isn't my preferred method of dying. Nevertheless, despite being nervous, I jumped at the chance. Part of my adventure into retirement is getting out of my comfort zone and trying new things.

The closer we got to "fish day," however, the more my mind would drift to visions of being stranded 12 miles offshore while clinging for life to an overturned boat as I fought to survive 80-foot waves kicked up by a heretofore unheard-of spontaneously generated hurricane. My fears grew by the day because every time I turned on the television I was guaranteed to come across at least one of the following movies: Titanic (both 1997 and 1953 versions), Perfect Storm and Jaws (I, II* and III). I thought God might be trying to send me a message, letting me know that the Grim Reaper was waiting for me off the Delaware shore. I considered backing out but then decided that if God really wanted me dead, he or she wouldn't pick something as elaborate as a fishing trip. Why go to such lengths? He could strike me down at any time with a lightning bolt, the bubonic plague or by lodging something as simple as a piece of ham sandwich in my throat until I choked to death. I decided the right course was to confront my fears head on and go fishing (although I did temporarily give up ham sandwiches).

So that's how I found myself with Rob pulling up at Greg's house on a Saturday morning at 4 a.m. Greg already had the 24-foot boat hitched to his truck. It looked enormous sitting on what had to be the largest trailer I've ever seen towed behind a truck. Looking at it I felt considerably more relaxed about venturing on to the ocean.

Two hours later, with one stop at a convenience store for breakfast where I bought two donuts, we reached the shore. The sun was just rising. The pink light reflected off the seagrasses and the hulls of boats in the marina. I stood to the side marveling at the beauty of the morning as Rob and Greg backed the trailer down the ramp. While they lowered the boat into the water, I couldn't help but notice that somehow, on the ride down, it had gotten smaller. Much smaller. It went from being this gigantic 24-foot boat on the back of a trailer to this tiny little vessel dwarfed by the mega yachts tied up in the marina. It didn't help knowing that the most treacherous part of the trip would be the first leg of our journey.

Indian River Inlet is legendary for its currents. At high tide, the back bay fills with millions of cubic feet of water, all of which flushes out at low tide through one tiny inlet less than 100 yards across. The result can be impressive. Just imagine the wave action in your toilet when you flush it and then multiply that by about a trillion gallons and you'll get the idea. I had some trepidation about this, particularly since one of my goals, aside from catching a fish, was to avoid throwing up on Greg's boat. I figured that barfing all over the deck would be bad form. Rob and Greg assured me that plenty of others had already done it, which was not an entirely comforting thought. To my relief, I made it through the inlet with my stomach intact. In fact, much to my surprise, I enjoyed the journey. It was an awesome ride. The kind of ride people will pay money for at an amusement park. The only problem with the channel cruise was that it was too short. Within minutes we had cleared the inlet and were on the ocean headed east, with the land quickly disappearing from view. About seven miles out, with just a sliver of land still visible on the horizon, we passed a cluster of boats clearly fishing for something. It looked like a good spot to me, but Greg kept going, moving past the little fishing ground, with its two- to three-foot swells, to a point far out on the horizon.

Actually, to a specific point on the horizon. Greg's boat was equipped with a top-of-the-line GPS system, which included a memory feature that recorded each spot in the ocean where he and Rob had caught flounder. While showing me the features of the GPS, Greg explained that the fish didn't have a chance. He made a very convincing case.

By the time we reached our destination, the seas were clearly angry, or at least annoyed. Three- to four-foot swells rocked our boat, but I felt okay. I didn't have the sea legs to move around the deck with anything approaching grace, but I wasn't throwing up, either. So far, I was achieving my first goal.

Rob showed me how to bait my line and went over the basics of flounder fishing, which essentially involves dropping a line rigged to an eight-ounce lead weight over the side and letting the weight bounce off the bottom of the ocean as the boat slowly drifts out to sea. Presumably, you either catch a fish on your hook or knock one out cold with the bouncing weight and hope it floats to the surface. Within minutes, I had my first action. The rod bent sharply, making an almost "U" shape. Line rocketed from the reel. Whatever it was, it was big! I struggled to stay ahead of the drag. There was great excitement on the boat until we all reached the inescapable conclusion that the only thing

I had hooked was the bottom of the ocean and no matter how hard I tried it would be impossible to pull it to the surface. Nevertheless, it put up one hell of a fight and it took considerable skill on Rob's part to finally free the line. I re-baited the hook and dropped it over the side, letting the weight bounce on the bottom and hoping for a real fish.

Then we waited. And waited. And waited.

As we sat on the boat, rocking up and down in four-foot swells with the sun mercilessly beating down on us, Rob told me an astonishing story about flounder. In my opinion, flounder are among the ugliest of fish. Most fish swim upright, in a vertical position, and have one eye on each side of their body. Many fish are beautiful, presenting vivid colors and patterns. Others are sleek, designed to glide through the water at great speeds. Some are awesome just because of their sheer size. Flounder are none of these. They live on the bottom of the ocean eating pretty much whatever sinks to their level. They swim flat to the earth and have both eyes on the upper side of their body. This is a neat evolutionary twist to help them capitalize on their niche environment as bottom dwellers. But here's the part Rob told me that I didn't believe until I Googled it (my apologies, Rob, for not believing you): Flounder are born looking like every other fish. Young flounder have one eye on each side of their body and swim vertically. As they get older, the right eye slowly moves to the left side of the head and the flounder begins to swim with its right side always facing the bottom and the left side facing up. The normal side-to-side movement of most fish is transformed into an up-

and-down movement in flounder. The sides of the flounder also change color to adapt to this bottom-dwelling life. Who (meaning you, God) would design a life cycle like this? Imagine if humans went through something along these lines? Picture yourself getting up one morning to discover that your right eye had moved a few inches toward the back of your head, beginning a journey that would eventually take it all the way around to the left side of your face. This would freak me out. I found myself feeling sorry for the flounder with its traumatic childhood. Puberty was bad enough. I don't think I could have dealt with total facial rearrangement.

As time passed, my empathy for the poor flounder was replaced with anger at them for not going after my bait. After all, they live on the bottom of the ocean. How picky could they be? Besides, they have two eyes on one side of their body. They couldn't claim not to see my bait. Not only that, but I had gone to the trouble of wearing my lucky fishing shirt. This was a brand new article of clothing I had picked up at Macy's specifically because it had images of fish printed all over it. I figured if I was going fishing, I should look the part. I wanted the fish to know I was serious about this endeavor. Yet they didn't seem to care at all. In fact, they seemed to be completely ignoring the three of us. And just as I was about to express my anger in colorful language, Rob hooked a fish.

There is an excitement to fishing that can't be denied. It's something primordial. It harkens back to our roots as early primates. We were catching our dinner. We weren't shopping at a Safeway or Whole Foods. No, we were hunters. We were a tribe of three waiting to find out what would emerge from the sea. In this case, it was a very nice 17-inch flounder. Dinner was ours!

We continued to fish for several hours while the tunes of our youth blasted on the stereo. We talked about fishing. We talked about politics. We talked about old friends and classmates. Mostly, we fished. Occasionally, we would move the boat into a new position and then let it drift across the prime fishing ground, guided all the way by Greg's GPS. Any concerns I might have had about being stranded in a small boat 12 miles out to sea disappeared as the day went on and as our fishing ground became increasingly populated with other boats. Eventually it became so crowded that I contemplated swimming over to a large cabin cruiser off our port side to see if I could use their bathroom, but decided it wasn't yet an emergency.

Rob caught another fish. It was too small to keep. Greg did the same before catching the largest fish of the day a few minutes later. This made me the only member of the tribe without a catch. And while I was feeling a little left out, it suddenly happened. I felt a hit on the line. I pulled back on the rod to set the hook. I felt the fish take off, putting up a struggle I can only compare to a Marlin or possibly a shark. I fought it for a full 30 seconds, maybe longer. Finally, it broke the surface and Rob netted it. I stood before them both while Greg snapped a picture of me and my sunfish-sized flounder, which had to measure at least seven or eight inches. I could not have been happier. I caught a fish! I had achieved both goals for the day.

In the end, we had two fish worth keeping. And, despite some sizable swells, I managed to keep my stomach in line even after Rob and Greg explained that donuts are probably the worst thing to eat before fishing (a heads-up would have been nice). I had a great time.

Later that afternoon, after Rob expertly cleaned and filleted the fish, his wife Ann was kind enough to cook them. They tasted great! Really, the best flounder I've ever eaten.

Rob and I are planning on doing it again. Next time, we're going to try fly fishing. I am looking forward to it! I hope to catch the biggest fly.

I watched them all, especially Jaws II—I love the scene where the shark eats the helicopter.

Secrets for successful travel

Ask anyone what they hope to do in retirement and nine out of 10 people will say they plan to travel more. Grand trips to wonderful places, whether across the world or across your state, are an almost universal dream among retirees. Sylvia and I are no exception. We love to travel. In retirement we hope to hit the road every chance we get, with each dollar we can afford and maybe with a few we can't.

Because travel is such a universal retirement dream, I decided it would be impossible to write about transitioning to retirement without a chapter on it. Omitting it would be like writing a book on French cooking without reference to butter or cream. It can't be done. The only problem was that I wasn't sure how to approach the topic. Sylvia and I one day plan to visit Australia and I thought I could write about that until I read Bill Bryson's "In a Sunburned Country" and realized that I could never write it as well as he did. Besides, any chapter documenting one trip might seem boring unless the reader were planning to visit the same country. After giving it a lot of thought, I decided instead to share my top 10 tips for travelers based on 30 years of experience.

1. Avoid strange bathrooms.

I am not a big fan of public toilets. This is especially true of men's bathrooms where you can always count on there being a puddle of piss collecting below every urinal and tiny splattered droplets of urine on every toilet seat. It's disgusting. Some men's rooms are so awful I've considered traveling as transgender just to be able to avoid them altogether. The only thing holding me back is my concern that Sylvia might freak out at seeing me in a dress no matter how valid the reason or how well I pulled it off.

If I am forced to use a public facility, I prefer airports where people go through high-level security screening before getting access to the restrooms. But sometimes when you gotta go, you don't have much of a choice. It's either a public lavatory or going outside to urinate and that's illegal in most places.*

Which brings me to my story ...

I was with Sylvia at Union Station in Washington, D.C., one early morning waiting for a train to Philadelphia. My bladder was approaching bursting stage. The public men's room was the only real option.

I was pleasantly surprised to find it empty and apparently recently cleaned. Before me stood a row of ten gleaming white urinals, all looking as inviting as the day they left the factory. Not a piss puddle in sight. I sauntered up to one near the far end of the row. As I was beginning to answer nature's call, I noticed another gentleman enter the room pushing a shopping cart that appeared to hold all his worldly possessions. He strolled down the line of urinals coming ever closer to where I was standing.

For women readers who may not be aware of this, there is an unwritten code when it comes to men's bathrooms. This code has been passed down from father to son for thousands of generations. It dates back to the very first caveman who took it upon himself to carve a crude urinal out of a block of stone. The code is very simple: You do not select a urinal next to an already occupied urinal unless there is no other possible option. There are no exceptions to this rule. Actual code violations are unheard of. They are rarer than verified unicorn sightings; rarer even than Donald Trump getting through an entire speech without insulting someone. In fact, they are so rare that there is no written guide as to what to do in case of a violation.

This didn't stop my new colleague from walking up to the urinal immediately to my right. He undid his belt, his button and his zipper and let his pants drop to his ankles. He stood there for a moment doing nothing, then turned his head toward me and asked, "Do you want to hold my dick while I pee?"

I could have responded with something clever like, "There doesn't appear to be enough to grab on to" or "I would if I could see it" or "You call that a penis?" Or I could have been truly snotty and replied with something sarcastic like "Do you want to wipe my ass after I take a shit?" Instead, I employed a technique perfected from 40 years of living in Washington, D.C. I ignored him.

Over the years, I've ignored hundreds of homeless people. It is not something I'm proud of. These are people who deserve compassion and, at the very least, some acknowledgment of their existence as human beings. But where I live, the daily onslaught of panhandlers quickly hardens even the most caring of hearts. I learned early on that engagement leads to interaction, which often leads to confrontation unless pre-empted through a gift of pocket change. Hence my strategy of non-engagement.

In this case, ignoring the homeless guy did not have the desired effect. In fact, it seemed to annoy him. I came to this conclusion because he continued to stare at me and then said in a voice that started as a whisper and quickly escalated: "I asked … Do ... You ... Want ... To ... Hold ... My ... Dick ... While ... I ... PEE?"

Before I could answer, he took it up several notches, yelling at the top of his voice, "DO YOU WANT TO HOLD MY DICK WHILE I PEE!

I looked at him and yelled back, "NO!" I meant it to sound firm. Instead it came out sounding more panicked than a pack of coastal townspeople fleeing a tsunami. Panic is never good. I know this from junior high. It's like pouring blood into a sea of sharks; you are likely to be eaten alive. I braced for the frenzy, ready for his next move.

"Okay, then," he calmly said. He then took his manhood in hand, pointed it toward his urinal and began to pee, letting out a noticeable sigh as he did.

I finished up, zipped up and got the hell out of there. Lesson learned. Avoid strange bathrooms.

As I wrote this, I began to wonder if it really is illegal everywhere. It turns out, at least according to the Internet, that in Britain it is legal for a man to urinate in public as long as it is on the rear wheel of his car and as long as he has one hand on the vehicle. The Internet did not explain why the law specifies the rear versus front tire or why you have to have just one hand on the car. I suspect this is one of those things you can only really understand if you are British.

2. Wherever you go, pack Cipro.

Sylvia and I often travel to some pretty dicey places where drinking the local water is considered tantamount to playing Russian roulette. So, whenever we travel, we pack a prescription for Ciprofloxacin (a.k.a. Cipro). Cipro is an awesome drug that I have used on several occasions to kill off more than one powerful stomach bug. It's the Atomic Bomb of antibiotics.

When my wife's cousin invited us to join her family for a trip to Disney World, I thought about packing Cipro but decided not to. We were, after all, going to Florida, not South Sudan. We would still be in the United States, where everyone knows the public water is drinkable (this was before Flint). What could go wrong?

We arrived in the Magic Kingdom on a Saturday afternoon and headed straight for the "World of Tomorrow." It was great, a flashback to my own childhood and what people in the 1960s thought the future would look like in the year 2000, which can best be described as molded plastics in every possible primary color. My excitement almost matched that of the thousands of small children running around in every direction.

Now here's the thing. Sylvia and I don't have kids. While I may have understood on a cerebral level that children are responsible for spreading more diseases than mosquitoes and rats combined, I didn't really believe it. And while I knew that their idea of proper hygiene is to wipe their noses on the backs of their hands and return to whatever they were doing, I was never told that their snot is toxic to all living things. I didn't understand the risks and the odds were decidedly against me. There had been probably 600 kids that day on the rides ahead of us, with each one carrying some deadly illness. I know because I caught them all. Although at the time it wasn't immediately apparent.

The World of Tomorrow was followed by dinner, where I ordered a gigantic, wonderfully greasy hamburger with all the fixings. I, of course, added fries on the side and washed it all down with a couple of beers. Later, as we walked along what are now known to be the crocodile-infested ponds of our Disney Village, I joined Sylvia and the others in ordering a large bowl of ice cream. All in all, it was a beautiful, magical evening at the magical kingdom until 3 in the morning when I magically started projectile vomiting. I'm not talking about a run-of-the-mill upset stomach. I'm talking about an astonishingly huge volume of stuff being ejected from deep within my body at speeds approaching the sound barrier. Over the next five hours, I became reacquainted with my dinner and ice cream along with every other piece of food or drink I had consumed for the past several years.

I spent most of the night with my head buried deep within the rim of the toilet. By the second hour, I was exhausted. By hour three, I was convinced that I was patient zero for some new virus slightly less deadly than Ebola or the Black Plague, and found myself wishing I had either of those because at least I could count on them to eventually kill me. By hour four, I was praying to God, asking him or her to put me out of my misery and welcome me through the Pearly Gates. My prayers were ignored.

The next morning, Sylvia found me lying on my back on the tile floor with a wayward clump of vomit serving as a pillow for my head. She sprang into action, proving yet again to be the caring, loving person I married. She took one look around the bathroom and slowly shook her head. From my vantage point on the floor, I couldn't at first make out what she was seeing, but when I rolled my head to the side it became apparent that I had missed the toilet on more than one occasion. In fact, the whole bathroom looked like the aftermath of a gigantic puke explosion.

She took all of this in and then said, "I told you not to order that hamburger."

I spent the next three days confined to the hotel room, never venturing more than 15 feet from my new bestie—the toilet. I'll never forget that commode and the times we shared. To this day, I wonder if it has ever forgiven me for all the abuse I hurled on it.

For those who have never experienced being sick at Disney World, let me assure you, there is nothing magical about it. The TV in my room had something like 40 stations, almost all of which were Disney programming. As a result, I not only spent three days sick in a hotel room while my wife and others went off and had fun, but I spent three days watching reruns of *Hanna Montana* and *The Suite Life of Zack and Cody*. And if this is any indication of just how sick I was, I kept watching *The Suite Life of Zak and Cody* because the show didn't make any sense to me. Who were these kids? Why were they living in a hotel? Why did the girl these kids seemed to have a crush on look about 20 years older than them? Why were they suddenly on a cruise ship? What happened to the hotel? Why weren't any adults taking care of them? And, most importantly, why were Zak and Cody so incredibly annoying? If I had been a member of the cast, I would have drowned both in the ship's pool on our first day at sea. None of it made any sense. That's why I preferred *Hanna Montana*. At least I could understand the plot. I was particularly moved by the episode in which Hanna gets a very large, unsightly zit on her face and learns that it's not what's on the outside that counts, it's what's inside. By the end of that episode I was moved to tears, although it might just have been the sweat pouring off my forehead from the 103-degree fever I was running.

By day four of our week-long vacation, I was feeling better. Not well enough to walk for hours around the Magic Kingdom, but well enough to get the hell out of the hotel, out of Florida and on my way home. I said goodbye to my wife, substituting a handshake for a kiss (not failing to notice that Sylvia subsequently doused her entire body in hand sanitizer), and caught the first flight I could out of Florida. I've never been back to the Magic Kingdom. More importantly, I've never traveled anywhere since without Cipro. Anywhere!

3. If you feel bird shit on the back of your neck, RUN!

One day, Sylvia and I were in Buenos Aires walking along a street near the presidential palace. Suddenly I felt something on the back of my neck. My hand instinctively reached back, returning with an indescribable yucky goop of some kind.

Fortunately, two middle-age women saw it happen. They ran over to help. One of them looked to the sky. My eyes followed her gaze. "Bird," she said in broken English. And while she was saying this, the other woman reached deep into her bag and produced some paper towels and a bottle of water. My angels of mercy started cleaning the back of my neck. They were so attentive. They had me bend over so they could more easily reach the back of my neck. Here I was, an

American, from a country that has probably screwed with their nation more than any other country, with the possible exception of Great Britain, and yet these people were helping me. I felt a warm feeling of gratitude that lasted about a half a second until things started moving very fast. Suddenly my wife had some bird crap on her as well. One of the angels stepped over to help her. Then I noticed a man out of the corner of my eye. Then I noticed that the man, who had a second ago been next to one of the ladies, was walking over to a cab. Then I put my hand where my wallet should have been but wasn't. Suddenly everything became crystal clear—we were being robbed. My angels of mercy were thieves.

I've been robbed plenty of times in my hometown of Washington, D.C., enough to be something of an expert. But I've never been robbed in a foreign country and I wasn't going to put up with it.

Out of the corner of my eye I noticed the guy getting into a cab. I took off after him, catching up as the taxi slowed to make a turn. I had no idea what to do or what I was doing but I was angry. Very angry. Without thinking I took my right foot and swung it as hard as I could at the door of the cab. Just as my foot was about to connect with the side of the car, and well past the point where I could stop its forward momentum, two thoughts passed through my mind at once:

1. I hope my thief is in that car; otherwise, I'm going to have a lot of explaining to do.

2. God, I hope that taxi keeps going because I don't want to confront an angry taxi driver along with a thief.

Fortunately, the cab took off in a cloud of burning rubber but not without a large dent in the passenger side door matching the imprint of my shoe. I may have lost a little money and a credit card, but as I watched the car drive off with the dent in its side, I couldn't help but feel a little alpha dog, even if it was an incredibly stupid thing to do.

We reported the crime to the police. They were very nice and very professional. They explained that the criminals use squirt guns to shoot the simulated bird poop. They said this kind of robbery happened all the time. They weren't kidding.

The next day my wife and I visited the botanical gardens. We were sitting on a bench when suddenly I felt bird shit on the back of my neck. I hate the feeling of being dirty. It brings back the horror of having to go camping with my parents every summer. Just as I was feeling completely grossed out, a nice gentleman came over and offered to show me where there was a water hose I could use to wash it off. I was ready to take him up on his kind offer to help until Sylvia shot me a look as if to say, "Are you out of your mind?" It was only then that I put it together and politely declined his offer.

A few months later I was telling my story to an acquaintance who had visited Buenos Aires before us. He told me he, too, had been robbed. We compared notes and determined we were robbed on the same street within a couple of blocks of each other by what were likely the same people. Small world.

4. Make friends with the locals.

Traveling is an opportunity to make new friends. Nowhere did that become clearer to me than during a cruise around the Galapagos Islands. This was one of the best trips Sylvia and I have ever taken, certainly in the top three, and one I would encourage anyone to go on if they can. I could write 50,000 words on why the Galapagos is so special, but here I'll just focus on one thing—the friends you can make, even those of an entirely different species.

Let's start with what I'll call "casual acquaintances."

In the Galapagos, cormorants have evolved into flightless birds that use their wings to propel themselves through the water at speeds fast enough to catch fish. Unfortunately, to achieve this impressive ability, their wings have evolved into short stubby things and they have lost the ability to fly. So what does a cormorant do when it is done fishing but finds itself a mile or two offshore? The answer, of course, is to seek help. On most days, as we tourists left the cruise boat and climbed into Zodiacs for the trip to shore, the cormorants would realize their chance had arrived for a free ride back to land. Cormorants are lazy but not stupid. One or two would jump onto the Zodiac, sit in the back of the boat and spread their wings to dry in the breeze as we motored in.

In between hiking around the islands, the Zodiacs would be used to take passengers on snorkeling expeditions. Galapagos is fantastic for its aquatic life. Even more impressive than the fish are the sea lions. Young sea lions like to play and have no fear of people. Most of them seemed to enjoy showing off their fancy underwater maneuvers to their human visitors. I could spend hours watching them, and often did, until the cold water would force me back onto the boat. During one trip, I was sitting on the edge of the Zodiac waiting to warm up enough so that my skin would change back from purple to tan when a sea lion jumped out of the water and took a position on the boat right next to me. We stared at each other for a while before he decided I was okay. Then he lay down and put his head against my leg. We sat that way for at least 10 minutes. I was both enthralled and terrified by the encounter. Sea lions have teeth, surprisingly large teeth, which he showed me each time he yawned. And while he didn't seem to have the slightest interest in chewing on me, I wasn't so sure that would be the case if I started moving around. I sat perfectly still until he decided it was time to move on. We parted friends. In fact, it is a friendship I'll never forget.

5. Remember to pack the things you'd never think to pack.

Peru is a beautiful country, rich in history, culture and natural beauty. However, Peru is apparently not wealthy enough to pay its oxygen bill. This oversight on the part of whoever in the Peruvian government is responsible for paying the nation's utility bills is immediately noticeable when you get off the plane in the city of Cusco. A short walk up the jetway left me gasping for air. A walk around the block at our hotel required several hours of recovery time.

Sylvia insists that the problem was not caused by failed payments to the local oxygen utility (as I theorized) but is the result of Cusco being situated 10,000 feet above sea level. Either way, the effect is the same. I spent my first day there lying in bed under a mountain of blankets shivering my ass off while my body adapted to the lack of oxygen. I was so desperate for relief that I tried the local coca leaf tea, made from the same plant cocaine is extracted from. Yes, it came to that. I was welcoming small doses of cocaine, risking addiction, in hopes of alleviating the pain. On several occasions that first day, my wife and I both availed ourselves of the bottled oxygen kept in the lobby of the hotel behind the registration desk. In all our travels, Peru is the only place we've visited where the hotels serve up hits of oxygen the way other hotels serve up complimentary coffee.

By day two, we both felt much better. By day three, we were back to normal. I'm not sure if this was because our bodies had finally adapted to this oxygen-free environment or whether the government finally paid its utility bill. Sylvia thinks it was the former. I think it was the latter.

When we got home, I ordered several small canisters of oxygen online (yes, you really can buy oxygen tanks made for backpacking). I keep these handy in case we decide to visit another country that might be behind on its utility payments.

6. Adapt to the local customs.

I've always found it odd that Italy, the country that invented indoor plumbing, could have so many public bathrooms that lacked toilet seats. I'm willing to go out on a limb and say that the bath in our hotel room may have been the only place in all of Rome where we encountered an actual seat on top of the toilet.

It wasn't clear to me whether toilet seats are considered a luxury in Italy or whether toilet seats are so rare that they are stolen within hours of being installed. I admit that at first I was put off by using toilets that did not have seats. I considered buying one at a hardware store (assuming they sell them) and carrying it with me wherever I went. I even toyed with the idea of turning a small profit by renting the seat out to other restroom users. In the end, though, I figured it would be too cumbersome to carry a toilet seat around and it would likely draw too much attention.

So I decided not to be the ugly American. I would adapt. Different country, different customs. And what I learned from this situation is that when you get right down to it, a toilet seat really isn't that necessary. Yes, a seat is more comfortable than sitting on the rim of the bowl, but in the end, either works.

7. Seek out the rare and unbelievable.

One of the greatest joys of traveling is when you come across one of those stories from history that is just too unreal to be believed—the kind of tale that is too scary, weird, stupid or creepy for even the most vivid imagination to conjure up.

I love these stories. So much of history is about war, disease, disasters and other calamities that, after a while, they pretty much sound the same, with just a small change in time and location. But every now and again you come across a story while traveling that is so over the top that it stands out like a diamond and is too precious to forget. These are the gems of traveling and I encourage you to seek out and collect them. Here are two of my favorites:

> **The Unsinkable William Clark.** I first heard of William Clark while visiting a museum in Canada. Clark was either one of the luckiest men who ever lived or one of the unluckiest. It's hard to tell which. Clark was unlucky enough to be hired on as a fireman to the Titanic before it sank on its maiden voyage on April 6, 1912. However, he was lucky enough to survive, somehow making his way into lifeboat 15. Two years later, he was serving on the crew of the Empress of Ireland. The Empress collided with another ship in the St. Lawrence River and sank in 15 minutes, taking more than a thousand lives with it. Clark again survived. There is strong circumstantial evidence that he may have gone back to sea a few years later under the name Frank Toner. It

is not hard to see why he might want to assume a new identity. After all, despite his own uncanny knack for survival, no captain in his right mind would want to hire someone as unlucky as William Clark. Sailors are a superstitious lot, and Clark was clearly jinxed. If the sinking of two ships were not enough proof of that, then consider this: Clark, masquerading as Toner, signed up to work on the Lusitania. The Lusitania was torpedoed during WWI by a German submarine off the coast of Ireland and went down in 18 minutes with a loss of 1,200 lives. Frank was one of 750 survivors. Clearly, God did not like William Clark or, depending on how you want to look at it, God really liked him. We'll never know which. Clark eventually took up farming. I can't say I blame him.

Pedro and Inez. The Alcobaca Monastery in Portugal is a beautiful church built in the 12th century. Despite its rich history, it is best known for one thing: being the final resting place for Pedro and Inez. Theirs was a tragic love affair with a particularly gruesome ending. Pedro was a young 14th century prince when he fell head over heels in love with Inez. They were the Brad and Angelina of their day, known in all the local pop-culture media as "Pednez."* Pedro's father, the king, disapproved. The king insisted that his son marry Constance, which he did. When Constance died, Pedro took right back up

115

with Inez. The king was not pleased by this. For whatever reason, the king *really* disliked Inez. His solution? Simple, really. He had her killed. This, I'm guessing, put a serious strain on the father-son relationship. Years later the king died and Pedro replaced him on the throne. Among his first acts was to have the beating hearts cut from the chests of each of Inez's murderers. Then he had her body dug up and crowned her queen in a lavish ceremony that included having everyone in the court kiss her decomposing hand while her body sat propped up on the throne. Pedro and Inez are buried in two magnificent Gothic tombs prominently displayed in the church.

* I made the "Pednez" part up but the rest of the Pedro and Inez story is true.

8. Hedge your bets; visit every church you can.

I am not a particularly religious person. To be honest, I'm not entirely sure which is the "true" religion. Worse yet, I don't care.

I was baptized as a Catholic. I learned the basics of Catholicism early on—guilt, fear, and the importance of placing unquestioning faith over any kind of logic or reasoning—but it never really took. And while I may be willing to stake my life on my beliefs, I'm not sure I'm willing to stake my eternity on them. That's why I've been hedging my bets.

When we travel, Sylvia and I make sure to visit all the best churches. This is particularly true when we visit Europe. My wife and I have been to Notre Dame, Chartres, Saint Peter's Basilica, La Sagrada Familia and too many other churches to count. Part of the reason we visit churches is that these beautiful buildings, whether Byzantine, Gothic or Romanesque, were the public works projects of their time. The wealth of a town would be recirculated as money donated by rich citizens went into the wages of carpenters, stonemasons and hundreds of other craftsman. These weren't the public works of today, where a bridge or building can go up in a year or two. These projects often took hundreds of years to complete. The sons, grandsons and great-grandsons of the initial workers became the generations of workers whose family roots quite literally dated back to the foundations of the building.

Another reason we make it a point to visit churches is the sheer awesome beauty of the structures. Everywhere you go in Europe, it looks like each town was trying to outdo the others, and that's because they were. One might argue that these Christians of the Middle Ages could have chosen more practical public works, like improving their roads or building sewage systems, but why would I travel all the way to Europe to see a medieval waste-water treatment plant? No, I think they made the right decision by focusing on art and architecture as expressed through their houses of worship.

The final reason we visit churches is, as I've mentioned, because I am hedging my bets. There is always a chance that everything in the Bible turns out to be true. If that's the case, I will, someday, find myself standing in front of the Pearly Gates while St. Peter makes his judgment. I could never get away with lying about my abysmal record of church attendance. Even trying to do this might be a tipping point regarding his decision on my eternal fate. But I might be able to get away with pointing out that while alive I actively sought out and visited as many of the great Christian churches of the world as I could, just to marvel at all that man has achieved when inspired by the Word of God. That should count for something, right? (NOTE: In the interest of full disclosure, to be on the safe side, Sylvia and I also have visited many of the world's greatest mosques. I mean, you never know.)

9. Never camp.

I know many people will disagree with me on this but my advice is never to go camping. I speak from experience. My parents dragged my sisters and me camping every chance they got. They said they wanted to "broaden our horizons" but I think they really wanted to show us how miserable life can be while, at the same time, providing us with a new appreciation of the comforts of home. It worked.

I will concede that in between setting up the tent and taking it down (which took hours) we probably saw many wonderful things on our trips, especially when we drove clear across the country and back. However, I don't remember any of them. What I do remember about vacations with my parents is the constant feeling of being dirty. This is, in part, a natural byproduct of camping, where I was constantly becoming "one with the earth below" (see chapter on yoga) whether I wanted to or not. It is impossible when camping not to become one with the earth. There is no place to sit—whether log, rock or picnic table—that doesn't already have a layer of dirt on it. There is no place to walk where your shoes aren't kicking up clouds of earth laced with microscopic spores and fungi. And you cannot cook a meal on a kerosene camp stove without some particles of dirt helping to season the evening's dinner. I connected so well with the earth that I spent most family vacations with a thick layer of it covering my whole body. By the end of any so-called vacation I looked like Pigpen from the Peanuts cartoon, and felt even dirtier.

My parents' cheapness made it even worse. Back then, most campgrounds operated on the theory that if you wanted to make the really BIG money, the best way to do so was to charge campers for hot showers. To get any hot water at all, you had to deposit a quarter into a contraption next to the shower and turn a knob to start the timer. One quarter bought you about five seconds of hot water and my parents firmly believed that a quarter's worth of water was more than enough money for any child. It wasn't. I was never clean, always emerging from the shower with half my body still covered in soap suds, which would eventually dry to a white crusty film that would settle in between countless layers of dirt.

If all this were not enough, keep in mind that tents do not have air conditioning. Most nights I would lie on top of my plastic air mattress, sweating myself to sleep as beads of perspiration rolled off my forehead, carrying with them a thin layer or two of dirt and leaving little trails of visible skin in their wake. I woke up every morning with so many sweat tracks crisscrossing my face that I looked like something out of a science fiction movie, and I would have to live like that until the next allotment of the precious shower quarter.

Throw into this mix long days of using public restrooms, pit toilets and campground facilities swarming with flies, blood-sucking mosquitoes and giant mutant moths that looked large enough to carry off small unwatched babies, and you'll get a clear picture of what much of my childhood was like.

My breaking point with camping came on July 5, 1979. I was camping with friends from college in Booth Bay, Maine. July is a popular time to visit Maine and we were lucky to get the last available camp spot. The evening of July 4 consisted of drinking a lot of beer and watching fireworks. It was beautiful. We retired late, after drinking even more beers. Somewhere around dawn I remember waking up from a dream in which I was floating on a vast lake. And when I opened my eyes, I realized that I was actually lying on my back in about eight inches of water with just the front of my face breaking the surface. I listened to the rain as it pounded against the sides of the tent, only then remembering that our campsite was at the very bottom of a gigantic gully and only then realizing the implications of that. I did not immediately get up. My head hurt too much to move. But as the water level rose, I had no choice. It was either get up or drown, and, as you know by now, drowning is not my preferred way to exit this earth. I crawled out of the tent and, in a scene reminiscent of the moment in *Gone with the Wind* when Scarlet O'Hara digs a tiny turnip out of the ground and proclaims, "As God is my witness, I will never go hungry again!" I turned my head to the sky. With the rain beating against my face and my clothes drenched, I looked to the heavens and proclaimed, "God-Damn-Jesus-Christ-Son-of-a-Bitch ... as God is my F#&king witness, I will never go camping again!" And I haven't.

10. Keep traveling.

The secret to staying young is to travel. There is a wonderful sense of adventure that comes from visiting just about anywhere in the world. Familiar surroundings are replaced by the possibility of new discoveries lurking around every corner. Customs and beliefs you've come to accept without question are challenged by new ideas and you end up stronger and wiser as a result. Even something as simple as sitting in an outdoor cafe in a foreign country on a warm afternoon doing nothing but drinking a glass of wine and watching the locals walk by can be a marvelous and memorable moment. That's how traveling keeps you young.

Bonus tip!

If you ever get the chance, I strongly suggest you visit the International UFO Museum in Roswell, New Mexico. It is unlike any other museum I've ever visited. It is housed in an old movie theater in the middle of downtown. The star attraction is life-size replicas of aliens and their spacecraft, which you can pose with for selfies. There are numerous dioramas of the crash site, built with plaster of paris and featuring the plastic army men and model trucks of my youth. The best part is that the army men are slightly out of scale with the models, making them appear as though they are an army of alien humans from another world.

The museum store is about a third of the size of the museum itself and is a great place to do all your Christmas shopping … although truthfully, I don't think Sylvia appreciated the alien earrings or the UFO glow-in-the-dark oversized T-shirt that I suggested she wear as part of a role-playing adventure involving a lonely astronaut and a beautiful alien princess.

Most of all, though, what I got from the trip was bragging rights. I may have driven seven hours out of my way to visit Roswell, but no one else I know can say they have been to the International UFO Museum. No one. And not only that. Now whenever anyone mentions the possibility of life on other planets, I can crash the conversation as the only "expert" in the room based on my extensive research from an afternoon spent at the International UFO Museum. My credentials speak for themselves.

Speed racer

Have you ever wondered what will happen to those huge retail malls when they are all forced to close because of competition from online shopping?

I certainly have.

Shopping malls are an important marker on the timeline of my life. The first indoor mall, the Southdale Center in Edina, Minnesota, opened in 1956, the year of my birth. Every year since, these gigantic temples of consumerism have sprung up from one end of the country to the other. They have aged along with me, going from new and exciting places to hang out as a teenager to essential places to shop as I grew older. And now they are dying out, killed off by the convenience and comfort of shopping from home.

These massive structures are a big part of the postwar contribution to society by my parents' generation. They gave the nation the equivalent of a new main street—a destination, a gathering place and a melting pot where the recently arrived could learn our country's consumer culture and values, like the importance of owning $200 sneakers, $125 T-shirts and jeans with pre-cut wear holes. Malls had an impact well beyond their size. But now, more and more are

123

closing each year. What is to become of these enormous buildings when they are no longer filled with the everyday necessities of life and the hordes of people seeking to acquire them? Will they literally be put out to pasture—torn down and returned to farmland—or left to decay as invasive plants slowly exploit every crack, turning parking lots into briar patches and buildings into ruins for future archaeologists to study?

I can accept that the change may ultimately be good, but it is a little unsettling to watch such prominent symbols of my youth become ghost towns.

Then I reminded myself that this is the United States of America, the greatest country on earth. No one is better than us at looking at a problem and seeing it as an opportunity to make money. Somewhere, I figure, there will be a group of college students sitting around their dorm or frat house smoking bowls of pot when one of them will look up and say, "I've got an awesome idea for making money out of all these malls." Maybe the idea will be to turn them into Airbnbs, or giant indoor pot farms or maybe even prisons. Who knows what the metamorphosis will be, but whatever it is, I was confident it would be great.

It turns out that I was right to have faith in American ingenuity. A few weeks ago I got a glimpse of the future. It is not a land of boarded-up buildings, but rather a story of renewal and rebirth. And it all happened because I ran out of vacuum cleaner bags.

I don't have one of those fancy bagless vacuums. I have a 50-year-old canister model inherited long ago from a dead relative. It works great and I plan to keep it. The only problem is that it can be hard to find the right replacement bags. The last place I bought them was in a Target store at an aging mall near my sister's house in Virginia. I figured that was as good a place as any to buy more, so I cruised out to the mall one afternoon only to discover that the Target no longer exists. Gone was the red bulls-eye logo. In its place, some brilliant entrepreneur has opened what may be the single coolest mall attraction in America—indoor electric go-cart racing! The track, which takes up half of the old store, is about a quarter-mile long with five or six hairpin turns and a couple of good straightaways. I stood in awe, watching, while at any given moment upwards of a dozen go-carts zipped around the track at speeds approaching 20 miles per hour. I accepted that I would never again be able to buy vacuum cleaner bags from this once mighty department store and would instead have to order them online, but it didn't matter. I was blown away by what had sprung up in its place. I was not alone. There was a long line of people, maybe 50 in all, waiting their turn to get out on the track. These were not just kids and not just men and boys. There were couples on dates, fathers with their children, one group of college drinking buddies who may have gotten an early start on the festivities, and a few people with dress shirts and ties who appeared to have come to work out some hostilities before returning to the office.

Every age group, ethnicity and gender was represented. I was not surprised. After all, who among us has not fantasized about driving a racecar? Which of us has not pulled out onto a crowded highway and longed for the opportunity to blow by every other car as though each were standing still? What suburban minivan owner has not at some point reveled in the satisfaction that comes from shooting past a sporty import? These are powerful feelings fueled by the need for speed and the need to win.

I'll admit that I may be more affected by these desires than most, but let's be honest, we all harbor them to one degree or another. I exorcise my demons by driving fast, well above the speed limit, especially on highways. As enjoyable as this is, I would love the opportunity to take it up a notch by testing my skills against other drivers. The problem is I have no desire to go 200 miles per hour on a NASCAR track. The risks are too high. I've seen the crashes on TV—cars slamming into walls and bursting into flames; cars rolling over half a dozen times before bursting into flames; and cars literally disintegrating mid-air into fireballs that rain burning shrapnel on the fans below. I may be crazy but I am not stupid. NASCAR and Indy-style racing are out. Anything that involves my car bursting into flames while I am in it is off the table. On the other hand, going 20 miles per hour in an electric go-cart seems like a perfect match between my desire to compete and my wish to avoid a crispy, flame-broiled death.

I had to try this.

A few weeks later I returned to the track, dragging my sister Karen and her husband John along with me. Inviting Karen was unfair. Some might even call it cruel. My sister drives through her neighborhood at speeds rarely exceeding 10 miles per hour. She is routinely passed by bikers as well as by joggers and, I suspect, even by the occasional power walker. She breaks for green lights on the chance they might turn red. She obeys all stop signs, waiting at least a minute to proceed even when there is no traffic for miles.

When she rides with me, she likes to breathlessly call out hazards like falling leaves, blowing trash or potential collisions with hyperactive squirrels. She also likes to stomp on an imaginary passenger side brake pedal whenever I exceed 40 miles per hour. She refuses to drive on any interstate highways because going that fast makes her uncomfortable.

I knew Karen would not enjoy go-cart racing, but bringing her along was sort of an insurance policy —a guarantee that there was someone on the track I could beat. She did not disappoint.

We went on a Wednesday morning, figuring that most kids would be in school and the place would be empty. Our assumption turned out to be wrong. The track was packed with kids—home-schoolers, we figured—and we had to wait more than half an hour for our race.

For $20, you got 14 laps, with each lap taking less than 30 seconds to complete, making the $20 worth about six to seven minutes of fun. I did the math. This meant the owners were pocketing at least $200 an hour for each cart on the track. My admiration for those who came up with this idea increased even further.

Go-cart racing begins with a safety video that stresses the importance of not running into other cars and not crashing into walls. To drive home the point, the video makes it clear that failure to heed these safety rules will result in being permanently banned from the track. One could argue that these restrictions take some of the enjoyment out of the race but, given the potential penalty, I decided it was best to play by the rules.

Following the safety video, we were off to get our racing gear. I was hoping for the complete Mario Andretti look—a crash helmet and full-body asbestos suit—but all I got was the helmet. When I asked the young man assisting us why there were no body suits, he gave me one of those "how-would-I-know" shrugs. I was going to point out that like e-cigarettes, cell phones and hoverboards, the carts' batteries might burst into flames at any minute—but realized he would see no humor in that.

The three of us, along with two other drivers, both women in their 20s, were assigned to the same race. The young women were ringers. I had seen them on the track earlier that morning. They were good, clearly worthy opponents! They were seated in the first two carts followed by John, me and then Karen. The carts sit just inches from the ground, which adds greatly to the feeling of speed but frankly made getting into them a little tough. For me, settling in behind the wheel was less about hopping into the cart and more like plopping into the seat, with the last few inches being a complete free-fall for my butt. I realized that getting out would be even more of a challenge and might well involve me having to roll out or ask for help. Once behind the wheel, though, I felt ready for action. I didn't have long to wait. With a wave of the flag, we were off.

Several things surprised me about cart racing. First, it requires a lot of concentration. Each turn takes focused attention to line up the best approach and find the cart's optimum speed for the curve. Holding this level of concentration for six minutes was tough enough; doing it for the hours required to complete a NASCAR or Indy race would seem impossible. No wonder they crash. Second was the strength required to turn the vehicle. Apparently I've gotten used to power steering. I quickly realized that if I am going to take this up as a hobby, I'll need to seriously intensify my workouts. Finally, what surprised me most was the number of times I went zipping past my sister. I expected to lap her once or twice, but six times seemed like a lot for a 14-lap race. And the weirdest part was that I kept passing her in roughly the same spot. This seemed to defy some law of physics.

Sadly, the race was over in what seemed to be less time than it takes to smoke a cigarette. Both young women finished ahead of us, having lapped both John and me once and my sister probably a dozen times. My best lap speed was 26.7 seconds, more than five seconds slower than the overall track record holder.

I accepted defeat gracefully. It was, after all, my first time on the track and I'd had a lot of fun. My sister didn't seem to enjoy it nearly as much as I did. I assume this was due to her poor performance. I'm considering getting her a gift certificate to the track for next Christmas. She needs to practice before we go out again.

I have three suggestions for the track owners.

First, they should have a senior citizen day. While I know I bring more experience to driving than many of the younger racers, they, especially those under 30, have a decided advantage in the weight department. I can't compete with a 100-pound, 24-year-old woman. I weigh almost twice that and my extra pounds clearly affected performance. If not a senior citizen day, then at least establish weight classes for racing.

Second, they should offer senior citizen discounts. Twenty dollars seems like a lot of money for each race. If movie theaters can offer senior citizen discounts, why not cart racing? I plan to write AARP about this, maybe even start an online petition.

Finally, they need to expand. Even with the track taking up much of the floor space of a former department store, it still seemed small. They should take over the entire mall and open a gigantic track, something that would allow racers to use central corridors as straightaways, combined with laps around the food court and a few ramps to get to the upper levels. There might even be an opportunity to combine cart racing with actual shopping. But I'll leave the details of that up to the next group of pot-smoking entrepreneurs to figure out.

A shoe bag future?

I'm not a particularly religious person, but every night before I go to sleep I pray to God that I inherited my father's genes.

My father smoked two packs of cigarettes a day for at least 50 years (he quit around age 70). He was also very fond of beer. His diet consisted of red meat, eggs, butter, coffee (lots of it) and ice cream. It was devoid of anything green. His idea of health food was a hot dog with sauerkraut. I can't remember him ever exercising for the sake of exercise. I can't remember him ever being sick. He never had joint replacement surgery. He never used a cane. And when he died at the age of 86, his mind was as sharp as when he was in his forties.

My mother, on the other hand, never smoked and never drank. By the time she turned 70, she had had two knee replacements and one hip. By 72, she was showing early symptoms of memory loss.

I expect that taking care of my mom will take up a lot of time in retirement. I base this on the realization that it already does. From talking with friends and colleagues I've learned that this is a common activity for people my age. Parental care is not a hobby of choice but one more of love or at least obligation. As complicated as this can be, I have it easier than most. I have two sisters who are full partners in this effort and my mother can afford to live in a nice retirement community. This is good, because if she ever had to move in with me, I fear I would end up killing her. I take some comfort, though, in knowing that no matter how bloody the crime scene or how strong the evidence, I would never be convicted of murder. Any jury of my peers would rule it justifiable homicide—especially if they knew my mom.

My mom has many wonderful traits, but if there is one not-so-wonderful trait that defines her more than any other it would be her unbelievable stubbornness. For as long as I can remember, and likely going back to her own childhood, my mother has never done anything that wasn't her idea. She holds strong, immovable positions on every topic, major or minor. She can outlast anyone in an argument, wearing down her opponents until they reach a point where they just don't care enough to continue the fight. It is inconceivable to her that she could be wrong. As a result, she cannot be reasoned with.

I can live with this and even try to find some humor in it. But memory loss takes things to a whole new level. No decision is final until it is executed, and often not even then. Bad decisions are devoid of rational explanation. Good decisions are few and far between. Every decision is excruciating.

All of this explains why persuading my mom to move from her home of 30 years to a retirement community is the single greatest achievement of my life. My sisters said it couldn't be done. They said I would never succeed. They clearly don't know me, appreciate my steadfast determination or understand that, like my mom, I can be as inflexible as a steel beam and as tenacious as a terrorist. I am my mother's son. I learned from the best.

But even I must admit there were times when I doubted my abilities.

The fight over the retirement community went on for more than a year. We tried emotional arguments. We tried logical arguments. My sisters and I shamelessly played the grandchildren and great-grandchildren card. We talked convenience. We talked security. We brought her brochures. We arranged field trips to retirement communities. Nothing worked. During one heated argument, I made the mistake of pointing out that it might be fun to have other people her age to hang out with, to which my mom said, "I don't like old people." To which I replied, "Neither do I." The conversation went downhill from there.

None of our arguments worked, or maybe they all did. I'll never know exactly why but one day Mom announced that she wanted to move. This is known throughout the family as the Christmas Miracle of 2013.

What my mother likes most about the retirement community is that it gives her an opportunity to complain. She'll happily tell any stranger we meet that I put her in "*that institution,*" then go on to describe its prison-like features. Truthfully, I wish it were a prison. I would love to have the peace of mind that comes from knowing that she has a free place to live, full government-paid medical care and, most importantly, a lockdown facility that won't let her wander off on her own. I've even tried to think up crimes I could frame her for, perhaps lending out her apartment to narco-terrorists or just turning it into a gigantic pot farm. I haven't done either, but only because I don't know any narco-terrorists and because the only thing I am capable of growing is bathroom mold.

Besides, jail would be a short-term solution at best. Even if convicted and sentenced to prison, she would quickly unify the screws and cons into petitioning the governor to grant her a pardon. Nothing brings people together like a common enemy.

When my mom talks about the institution where she is incarcerated, she conveniently leaves out details, like her cell being a beautiful one-bedroom apartment, with meals not delivered through a slot in the door but instead served in any of three restaurants where she selects a three-course meal from a menu. She also conveniently leaves out any mention of the swimming pool, workout room, free shuttle bus to local stores, on-site medical care and a hundred different activities, none of which she participates in.

I have overheard her tell people when she thinks I'm out of earshot that she likes the retirement community. She has never said that to me. I don't want her to. I am concerned that if she ever did, hell would freeze over. I don't want that to happen. No one knows the long-term ramifications on global climate change if the molten core of the earth suddenly were to turn into a giant ice ball. I'm not willing to take that risk.

My mom is 85 now. I believe that what keeps her going is a lifelong commitment to driving everyone crazy. Do I wish she had a different hobby? Of course, but I'm also glad she has something to keep her going —a reason to get up in the morning. I hope that when I am her age, I have so much purpose in my life.

Despite our mother's challenges, my sisters and I do love this increasingly crazy woman and we are committed to making her remaining years as comfortable as possible. We owe her that much and, truthfully, much more. Toward that end, we have only three goals:

1. Get her to wear new shoes.

My mom has been wearing the same pair of sneakers for 10 years. This would not bother me were it not for the gigantic hole that runs the full length of the side of the right sneaker. The solution would seem simple: Buy a new pair of shoes. But nothing is simple with my mom. By my count, she has at least a dozen new, never worn, pairs of shoes. She claims none of the new ones are comfortable. We've tried sandals, sneakers and slippers to no avail. We've tried walking shoes, running shoes and shoes of every type, color, size and shape. We've even tried boots. My mom won't wear any of them. Every birthday, another pair is added to the closet-of-never-worn shoes.

I once pointed out to Mom that her feet would get wet if she wore the holey sneakers out in the rain. That's when she explained her "shoe bag" technique. It goes something like this:

1. First you put on socks.
2. Then cover the socks with plastic bags from the supermarket.
3. Then slide your foot with the bag into the shoe.
4. Lace them up and you are good to go.

Here I was thinking that my mom was becoming a little crazy, but who can argue with that kind of ingenuity? It forced me to see her in a whole new light. She's not a weird, old lady with a memory issue and some unnatural relationship with a 10-year-old pair of sneakers that smell worse than the boy's locker room in any American high school. Instead, she's an inventor!

I have come to accept that I will never get her out of those shoes. I plan to bury her in them. Better yet, I think I'll bury her in one of the new, uncomfortable pairs. Let her wear those for all eternity. Revenge is sweet!

Of course, this assumes I outlive her. No guarantee on that.

2. Get her to wear new eyeglasses.

I was with my mom when she broke her eyeglasses. I can still picture it in my mind. The whole scene plays back like a slow-motion horror movie, starting with my mom taking off her glasses and moving to lay them on the counter. Next comes an anguished cry from me as the frames strike the counter and snap in half. This is followed by a close-up of the right lens popping out and taking flight, then a hard cut to me diving across the room to catch the lens before it hits the floor and shatters.

At that moment, I knew a significant part of my life was over. Gone would be my leisurely exploration of retirement activities. In its place would be hundreds, if not thousands, of hours spent obtaining new glasses for my mother. At the time, I didn't know exactly why it would be so difficult to achieve something that should be so easy. I just knew it would be.

If my career has taught me anything, it has taught me how to break down any problem into tasks and to build an action plan around each one. I applied these skills to this problem and came up with a short outline of what needed to be done:

1. Temporarily put lens back in frame and hold in place with tape
2. Get eye examination
3. Pick out new frames
4. Order glasses
5. Pick up glasses

I'm going to spare you the blow-by-blow account. Suffice it to say that six months later, we have now been through ...

- Three ophthalmologist appointments

- Three expensive new pairs of glasses
- Countless fittings

... and Mom is still wearing her original broken glasses held together with tape.

Somehow, though, just detailing the process doesn't really capture the pain. I've been with my mom as she has tried on every frame in the eye doctor's office two or three times while asking the nice sales people over and over why she can't get frames just like the ones she has. The answer is the same in each shop we've visited—"because they don't make them anymore"—but that doesn't stop her from asking the question again and again. I was with her when she loudly accused the doctor's staff of breaking her glasses in the first place because they obviously wanted to get her to buy a new pair. I cringed when my mom mocked the accent of a very nice clerk who was trying to help us. And I have no doubt that when asked about her broken glasses by other residents at the retirement community, she tells them that her children simply refuse to help her get a new pair.

This is one problem, though, for which I have found a solution: I have turned the whole thing over to my sister Karen to deal with. Good luck, Sis!

3. Get her to take her medications.

My mom takes four pills a day—or, more precisely, she *should* be taking four pills a day. Unfortunately, she doesn't remember to take her pills. I know this because I count her pills. I am not alone in doing this. My sisters have counted the pills. The doctor has counted the pills. The social worker has counted the pills. The occupational therapist has counted the pills. We have all come to the same conclusion—she takes about half of what she is supposed to. When confronted with evidence of this problem, my mom simply dismisses it by saying that we clearly "don't know how to count" because she takes her pills every day and then marks "it on the calendar."

Of course, she does neither.

There are half a dozen ways to solve this problem. I know because I've tried them all. All have failed.

We started with a pill tray. A simple solution, really. The pills go into a tray marked with each day and you take them on the right day. What could be easier? I use one. Sylvia uses one. Everyone I know uses one. They are simple and effective. However, a pill tray only works if it is used and my mom refuses to use one. According to her, "I've been taking pills out of the bottle since I was 13 years old and I'm not going to change now!"

Next we tried an automatic pill dispenser. I loved the pill dispenser, which, because of its shape, we referred to as the flying saucer. This is a wonderfully ingenious device. You load it up with 30 days of pills. Then each day, at a selected hour, it presents a little tray, dispensing the right pills. It also sounds an alarm to remind anyone within a 15-mile radius that it's time to take the pills. I figured the flying saucer was foolproof. How could it not work? If

Pavlov could train each of his dogs to expect food at the sound of a bell, I could surely get my mother to take her pills at the sound of the alarm. The flaw in my thinking, of course, was overlooking the fact that my mother is far cleverer than I give her credit for. Instead of taking her pills from the flying saucer, my mom would simply dump them onto the counter in an ever-growing pile. When asked why she would not use the flying saucer, Mom would revert to the same argument: "I've been taking pills out of the bottle since I was 13 years old and I'm not going to change now." I pressed the point and, in a moment of weakness, she told me the real reason. She is convinced that my brother-in-law is trying to kill her by giving her the wrong pills. I will admit that after a really bad day dealing with Mom, a small part of me might cheer him on. But he is not trying to kill her! My brother-in-law is one of the nicest people on the planet. He's a good husband and a good father, a good grandfather and fun to hang out with. I don't see him trying to poison my mom. Besides, as I pointed out to Mom, HE HAS NEVER FILLED THE PILL DISPENSER! EVER! This argument, of course, did not work. Facts have no relevance in her world.

Eventually, I gave up on the pill dispenser. If my mom was determined to take pills from a bottle, I was equally determined to find a way to make that work. I used a web service to set up an automated reminder call to her each morning at 8. The call came complete with a recorded message to "Take your pills now, you crazy old lady" (actually, I left the last four words off the message). I spent a considerable amount of time congratulating myself on my cleverness. How could this not work? The only problem was that it didn't. Somewhere between the phone and the pill bottles, my mom would forget.

Yet, I was not willing to let go of the basic idea. So my sisters and I killed the auto call and instead divided up each day of the week, with one of us calling her every day to remind her to take the pills. We would stay on the line as she took them. Later counts revealed that my mom had outsmarted us again. She merely pretended to take the pills when we called. She is nothing if not cunning.

Enter Edna.

Edna is about five feet tall and weighs a little under 300 pounds. She is close to my age, with jet-black hair done up in a set of permanent curls, a style she probably first adopted during the disco era and maintains to this day.

I love Edna. My mom hates Edna. I love Edna even more *because* my mom hates Edna. I'd marry Edna if I wasn't already married for no other reason than it would probably kill my mom. Edna is patient and sweet. I found her online. She provides a very special personal service. She stops by my mom's apartment every morning at 8 and sits with my mom while she takes her pills. After Edna leaves, my mom calls and yells at me, letting me know in no uncertain terms how much she hates Edna. She usually hangs up on me but calls back six or seven times to have the same one-sided conversation, each one ending with her hanging up. To this day, I can't tell if she repeatedly calls me because she can't remember that she called me a few minutes before or whether she is trying to drive home the point.

I don't think Edna will last. Eventually my mom will figure out that she doesn't have to open the door to let her in. I'm hoping that secretly my mom likes having someone help her and just doesn't want to admit it. But I doubt it.

The thing I have figured out about dementia is that it takes the best of a person's personality first. It is both hard not to feel sorry for my mom and hard to feel sorry for her. With a little effort, she could make life so much easier for herself and those who love her.

But she won't because she can't.

The disease responsible for her memory loss has taken away much of her ability to reason. What's left are the traits that have always made her challenging.

I've seen with my father that some people grow old while retaining their independence and the full range of their character. I've seen with my mom that the opposite is also true. While lifestyle choices may be a factor, sometimes it just comes down to the luck of the genes.

Hence my nightly prayers.

Write the great American novel

I wrote my first book about 15 years ago. At the time, I swore never to write another (obviously a promise I didn't keep). I know that a lot of people think about writing the great American novel in retirement so I thought I would share what I learned from that first experience.

My first book was a murder mystery. In the beginning, it seemed like a great idea—something that might be a lot of fun. Besides, I thought, what do I have to lose?

The answer to that question turned out to be about a year of my life. That's how long I spent secluded in my study every evening banging out a couple of thousand words and endlessly editing the same pages over and over and over and over again and then editing them a few more times. Eleven months, ten days and seven hours later (or something close to that), I emerged from my self-imposed solitude with completed murder mystery and the firm conviction that I would never, ever try to write another book.

Here's what I learned from the experience:

Writing a novel is all-consuming. It takes over your life. Wherever you are and whatever you are doing, you are thinking about your book. Usually, it was big picture stuff. "If I *were* to commit a murder, *who* would I kill and *how* would I do it?" This was a fun exercise until I realized that my list of potential victims was getting too long and the imagined methods of disposing of them were becoming far too graphic and inventive (i.e., would it be possible to slowly disembowel someone using nothing more than toenail clippers; how long would they suffer before they finally bled to death; and, most importantly, would they suffer enough?). Often the focus would be on more mundane aspects of the plot, like wondering if my characters would ever go to a Starbucks and, if so, would they be more likely to order the double latte espresso cappuccino or the espresso cappuccino double latte? The answer turned out to be neither since my book ended up being set in the early 1980s, long before Starbucks became a national phenomenon.

Dwelling on the plot and characters was not all bad. I tend to have a touch of obsessive compulsive disorder. When you are lying wide awake late at night, it's much more fun to be thinking about your characters and plot than worrying whether you left the stove on and debating whether to check on it. (Of course, you have to get up and check; how else are you going to get any sleep?)

Your characters take on a life of their own. A friend who is a successful author warned me about this phenomenon. After a while your characters become very real and start doing unexpected things that help move the plot along. At one point, two of my characters decided to sleep together. I never saw it coming. Of course, I had no choice but to write it down … every steamy word of it … even if some of their sex was a little disturbing ... even if some of it was so creepy I had to cut it from the final version.

I felt bad when the 20-year marriage between two other characters fell apart. How I wish they had been able to work it out—if only I could have been there for them! I felt even worse when another character tried to kill the heroine. Over and over I kept asking, "Why?" Finally I had to accept that every aspect of this scary, low-life murderer came from me. That realization nearly sent me into therapy.

Even more disturbing, though, was discovering that the characters were becoming more interesting than my real friends. My characters were having affairs. They were killing each other. They were making love on the pages in front of me. None of my real friends did any of that.

Eventually my characters started coming to work with me. We would regularly meet in the lunchroom to discuss their relationships and figure out what they were going to do next. Some of my flesh-and-blood colleagues expressed concern. I made a point of introducing them to my book concept and my new imaginary friends. I took great pains to reassure them that my friends, like me, were harmless except, of course, for the deranged killer among us. Part of me was hoping this would lead to an early retirement offer. It didn't.

You will come to hate your book. My advice to anyone who wants to write a novel is to start with the first page. If you can get one page done, you can assuredly do 10 pages. And if you can do 10 pages, there is no question you'll be able to finish a chapter. And if you can do one chapter, you can do lots of chapters. But keep this in mind—by chapter five you'll hate your book. You will have edited your pages so often that a mere glance at your work will cause your stomach to turn. By chapter 10, you will hate your book more than you hate every injustice ever bestowed on anyone in the world and you will curse your first-grade teacher for having made you learn the alphabet. By chapter 15, you'll be damning your parents for having conceived you and you will find yourself repeatedly calling your aging mother to let her know that.

By then it's too late to stop. You are too close to the finish line—the last period on the last sentence in the last paragraph.

Don't take my word for any of this. Here's what Winston Churchill had to say about the writing process:

"Writing a book is an adventure. To begin with it is a toy and an amusement. Then it becomes a mistress, then it becomes a master, then it becomes a tyrant. The last phase is that just as you are about to be reconciled to your servitude, you kill the monster and fling him to the public." (real quote)

Here's my attempt to outdo Winston Churchill. Pretty ballsy to try to outdo Winston Churchill but here goes:

"When you begin writing your novel, it is like a grand and glorious love affair. Every day is spring, the blossoms are always in bloom and your betrothed is always beautiful and alluring. By the end of the book, it's like a bad marriage —one you stay in only because the sex is occasionally good."

Your friends and family will come to hate you. If you are as fortunate as I am, you have wonderful friends and a loving family. These are people who have seen you at your best and worst. They love and respect you, and you love and respect them. They would be willing to do just about anything for you … up to a point. For most of my friends, that point came the third time I asked them to reread chapter one and tell me what they thought of it. My siblings, people I have known and loved all my life, began to bail around chapter six. Even my wonderful wife reached her breaking point on the 21st edit of chapter

10. After that I was alone, just my characters and me. I was okay with this. In fact, while sitting alone in my study night after night, I began to question whether I could trust my friends and loved ones. Were they saying nice things because they really liked the book or because they didn't want to hurt my feelings? Were their occasionally unkind comments rooted in valid criticism or were they jealous that I was clearly going to win a Pulitzer Prize and they weren't? As the book dragged on, I began to resent them for being able to live rich, full lives while I was shackled to a 75,000-word monster that still didn't have an ending.

In talking to other authors, I've learned that the loss of friends and loved ones is a common experience. It's why books are published with dedication pages. The dedication provides an opportunity to apologize to everyone in your life and thank them for caring enough to arrange the intervention.

You will learn to accept rejection. The truth is that my goal in writing the novel was always modest. I knew from Day One that I was not going to win a Pulitzer Prize or an Edgar Award. But I did have a dream. I wanted to see one person, *just one person*, somewhere—whether on a plane, a bus or on the beach —reading my book. Just one random person who would be holding the book in front of them and be so deeply engrossed that they would be completely oblivious to the happy dance I would be performing a few feet away. But to realize my dream, I had to be published, and that is a nightmare all its own. Hundreds of query letters to agents led to hundreds of rejections. I had serious interest from one New York agent, only to have it fall apart when the agent was laid off because of the disruption in publishing caused by e-books.

But e-books also have created an incredible opportunity for aspiring authors to get their works in front of the public. My book, *A Simple Murder*, by Lawrence Doyle, is available on the Kindle (please go buy it and write a review). To be honest, I haven't made a lot of money. I calculate I'm netting about 13 cents an hour when you compare what I have earned to the time it took to write the book. I obviously have a lot to learn about marketing in the digital world. That's okay, though, because the goal was never money. Nowadays, every time I get on the subway I take great comfort in knowing that the person sitting across from me deeply engrossed in their e-reader could be reading my book—MY BOOK! Happy dance time!

If you are reading this chapter, then you know that despite having sworn never to write another book, I am at it again. Somehow it seems more fun this time. So far, I'm really enjoying it. Of course, I'm not done yet. I'll check back in with you toward the end of the book.

Gambling with the future

It was my first time. I was young, maybe all of 19, not experienced in the ways of the world and certainly not ready for the harsh realities of being out on my own. Technically, I wasn't of legal age but that was the last thing I was worried about. To hell with age limitations. I was on a mission. I had to meet a lady—a very special lady, in a very special place.

There are probably hundreds of people arriving in Las Vegas every day who are down on their luck. Back then, I was one of them. I had $30 to my name, a quarter tank of gas and a 10-year-old car that showed every hard mile it had traveled. It was held together by rust, Bondo and a liberal application of muffler patches that covered most of the holes in the exhaust system. Those that remained made the car sound great, like I had a 500-horsepower engine under the hood of the powder blue 1965 Plymouth Valiant. The only problem was that I had to keep the windows rolled down to vent the fumes; not that much of a problem really since the car didn't have air conditioning and rolling up the windows would have brought about a quick death. It was late August and the city felt like the crust of the earth had opened and big chunks of the netherworld had escaped to engulf the surface.

I heard somewhere that everyone in Vegas has a story. If you ask me, I'd say everyone in Vegas has a problem. I know I did. Thirty dollars was nowhere near enough to get all the way from Nevada back to college on the East Coast. It looked like my only real option was going to be to call my parents collect and ask them to wire me some money. I didn't want to make that call. For one thing, it was embarrassing to be 19 years old and tapping my parents for cash. For another, I was dreading having to tell them I was in Vegas. This, I figured, would come as a surprise to them since I hadn't mentioned I was going on a trip—a slight oversight on my part for which I would now pay dearly.

They would be pissed, but I had a plan.

I drove around Vegas for a while, burning up precious fuel while looking for just the right place for that special encounter. I passed on the glitzy casinos along the strip, each with their neon lights beckoning me. None of them seemed right. Like the car, I was showing a lot of hard miles. I was in no shape for any place where the other patrons routinely showered. Besides, I figured it didn't matter where I ended up. If she was interested, she would find me.

My plan was simple. I put 10 dollars in my back pocket, held in reserve, to pay for the campsite that night, a little food and a pack of smokes. The remaining 20 was for gambling. The goal? Win enough to get home.

On the edge of town I passed a gigantic neon cowboy standing off to one side of the highway, his right arm mechanically swinging back and forth while holding a flashing deck of cards. He was clearly intent on sweeping drivers off the highway and into the parking lot. I accepted the invitation.

I pulled into a spot, shut off the engine and waited while it ran for a few more seconds until letting out a wheeze followed by a shudder that rattled the whole car, then finally finishing off with a loud clunk that always left me wondering if the engine would ever turn over again.

A Sinatra tune was playing on the sound system as I walked through the front door. Occasionally I could make out a note or two before the song would be drowned out by whistles and bells from the slot machines and the rattle of thousands of coins carried around in hundreds of plastic cups. The main room was filled from one end to the other with an enormous blue haze, the accumulated smoke of every cigarette burned there over the past 20 years. It hung from the ceiling like a massive storm cloud waiting to drop a world of hurt on the people below. The fluorescent bulbs, barely visible through the fog, flickered like tiny little bolts of lightning, almost unnoticeable when mixed with the flashing lights of the slot machines that fired off whenever a customer hit a jackpot. Taken together, the whole thing was horrible, like a sneak peek at hell.

This was the first time I'd ever gambled in a casino. I had a lot riding on the night. I headed straight to the $2 blackjack tables and proceeded to lose my $20 in what seemed like less than 10 seconds. My fate was sealed. I would be phoning my parents in the morning to ask them for money. I walked out thinking about that humiliating call. Halfway to the car, I stopped and turned around. I still had $10 in my pocket, and as long as I had money, I had a chance. I walked back into the casino and sat down again at a $2 table.

That's when I met her—Lady Luck.

My $10 quickly grew to $20, then to $30, and on to $50 and, in what seemed like less time than it took to lose my initial stake, I had $140 in chips in front of me. It was enough to get home. I wasn't going to risk it by getting greedy. I kissed Lady Luck goodbye. Ours was to be a brief affair but one I'll never forget.

Somehow I've always known I would never meet her again. For whatever reason, she had smiled upon me in my hour of desperation. It would be wrong to ever expect more.

I've been to a few casinos since then, never gambling much and never winning. Over the years, though, I've noticed three big changes since my earliest experience in Vegas. First, in most casinos the smoke is gone; outlawed by a government intent on protecting people from nicotine addiction but perfectly okay with casinos popping up on every corner, outnumbering even Starbucks in some places. Second, the buckets of quarters have been replaced with computerized slot machines that spit out paper receipts. And finally, in perhaps the biggest change of all, casinos are now filled with old people, really old people. It is hard to walk into any of them without noticing that gambling has become a big pastime for retirees. I don't fully understand the attraction but decided that in the service of this book, I needed to figure it out. I could think of no better way to do this than to call my retired friends, David and Gary, who are known to "occasionally" gamble.

David and I talked about going to Vegas or Atlantic City but decided on a casino half an hour away in suburban Maryland. David assured me, based on his own experience, that this is where the retirees hung out. He insisted we go on a Tuesday, saying Tuesdays at the casino always made him feel young and spry. I had a hard time making a connection between a specific day of the week and its effect on David's feeling of youthfulness and vitality until he explained that on a Tuesday, we would be among only a handful of patrons not dragging around personal oxygen tanks. He never explained why Tuesday was special for this subset of retirees but I assumed it was some kind of casino promotion, like "bring an oxygen tank and get a free refill."

David also insisted that we had to stay for the lunch buffet. According to him, the buffet was "great." His only complaint: "There is too much food and none of it is any good." Gary added that I would never forgive myself if I missed "the senior citizen version of the high school cafeteria."

In the years since losing my gambler's virginity, I've been back to Vegas a few times for work. I don't like the city but must admit it is a wonder to behold. The architecture is so over the top that you don't have to like it to be amazed by it. Each hotel tries to outdo the other in a quest to attract the most gamblers. The more elaborate and ostentatious, the better. Nowhere else on the planet can you find a 30-story pyramid a few doors away from a re-creation of Venice.

By contrast, the casino in Maryland wasn't trying to outdo anything, not even the shopping mall next door. It looked like the architect had made every effort to spare every penny. The result was a monolithic, square building that was little more than a five-story parking garage with a casino on the first floor. I've been in Walmarts with more panache.

As David and I waited in the lobby to meet up with Gary, we watched bus after bus stop long enough to disgorge 30 to 40 senior citizens. It was 10 in the morning and the place was filling up like a rock concert. The unending stream of people left me wondering how it was even remotely possible for Donald Trump to lose money in the casino business. The place looked busier than a Best Buy on Black Friday. It made me wonder if Social Security checks had just been mailed.

To be fair, David greatly exaggerated the number of oxygen tanks, but the presence of hundreds of senior citizens, many with walkers, gave the casino the look of an assisted living facility minus the nurses.

These were not the "young old," and I suspect most were arriving by bus because they had long since given up driving. It was a depressing view of the future, one that made me want to reconsider my decision 25 years ago to give up smoking. Then I would notice someone wheeling around an oxygen tank and remember why I did.

My strategy was to try all of what the casino had to offer, starting with blackjack, moving to slots and finishing with roulette.

I found one of the few remaining seats at a $15 blackjack table. This seemed like a lot of money to wager on each hand, at least until I realized that the guy next to me—who was one of the youngest people in the place—was placing $200 bets and playing several hands at once.

I held steady with $15 bets and was slowly winning. As my pile of chips grew, I couldn't help but notice that the young man next to me was having the opposite luck. His stake had diminished to what appeared to be less than a thousand dollars. I heard him tell a friend he was down more than $6,000 altogether. He didn't seem that upset. I would have been horrified if I was down $6,000. I'd have been visibly sweating while pounding on my chest with both hands to keep my heart from failing. The young man showed none of these symptoms, leaving me to wonder what kind of job he might have that losing $6,000 didn't seem to be a big deal. Not to mention what kind of job let him go gambling at 10:30 on a Tuesday morning. At first I thought he might be a drug dealer. This made sense to me. Maybe his job was to go to casinos and launder money. But then I noticed he looked a lot like Mark Zuckerberg, founder of Facebook. It seemed improbable but why not? Maybe Mark Zuckerberg has a gambling problem and prefers obscure casinos in suburban Maryland to the ritzy clubs in Vegas where he would surely be recognized? Maybe this was Mark's way of blowing off steam? I was about to snap a selfie of me with Mark to post to Facebook when I heard one of his friends refer to him as "Frank." I went back to my drug dealer theory.

Over time, Frank's fortunes turned around. His small pile of chips began to grow into an enormous stack. That's when something weird happened—the dealer stopped dealing, looked at Frank and suggested he leave. Frank replied that he was still down a thousand dollars and wanted to get back to break-even.

The dealer, in what I can best describe as sound fatherly advice, said to him, "Dude, I've been working here a long time. No one ever gets back to break even. The smart play is to take those chips, cash them in and leave."

Frank didn't take his advice. In no time at all the kid was back down to about a thousand dollars. I left. I didn't want to see how this ended. Besides, it was time to meet David and Gary for lunch.

David was right. The buffet was great despite there being too much food with none of it being very good. It was, however, a cut above the high school cafeteria of my youth just by virtue of having fresh fruit and a salad bar. But the overall ambiance, other than the average age and the significantly lower odds of a food fight breaking out, was pretty much the same.

It was loud, owing not only to the sheer number of senior citizens dining there but also to the number who seemed to be yelling to be heard over the seniors at the next table who were yelling because friends at their table were all hard of hearing. David, Gary and I found that by yelling ourselves, we not only could catch up on the latest happenings in our lives but also add greatly to the overall volume. We finished lunch with a quick report out. David was up about $200, Gary $300 and I was up $160. Gary had the common sense to leave immediately after lunch. David and I didn't.

My afternoon strategy was to hit the slot machines. The question was, which ones? By my estimate, 80 percent of the casino floor was taken up by slot machines. There were hundreds to choose from and no instructions I could find anywhere to help determine which machine was most likely to pay off. I walked the aisles, waiting for one to speak to me, like in a Twilight Zone episode I saw as a kid. It never happened. Apparently, real slot machines aren't well versed in the conversational arts.

I eventually decided to play only those machines where the theme was based on places I've visited around the world. I started with the very colorful "Galapagos Islands." To be honest, the machine didn't make a lot of sense. I couldn't figure out why three marine iguanas and two Dodo birds paid out more than three Dodo birds and two iguanas or why cute little penguins didn't pay out anything even if four of them lined up in a row along with what appeared to be a dancing hammerhead shark. I wondered if any one of the hundreds of people around me could explain the logic behind the payoff combinations. I looked for someone who appeared friendly enough to ask and came up empty. Most players seemed to be in a deep trance, as if trying to affect the outcome of each wager through sheer power of concentration. Or, and I'm not ruling this out, they were robots planted by the casino to bolster the notion that playing slots was fun and profitable. Either way, I decided it was best not to disturb them.

My next stop was a slot machine that attempted to faithfully recreate the tragic eruption of Mount Vesuvius that wiped out Pompeii and most of its residents in the year AD 79. I had to stretch things here a little. I was not in Pompeii when the volcano erupted but did visit the site 1,922 years later and figured that was close enough. I commend the makers of the slot machine for doing an excellent job of depicting the horror of that tragic event. Above the digital facsimile of a spinning wheel sat the image of an enormous volcano with fleeing Pompeiians beneath it. Each time I won, a simulated lava flow would emerge from the top of the mountain. The bigger the win, the more lava would rain down upon the doomed residents. It was a great machine. It provided a lot of entertainment but sadly very little cash. I moved on.

Location-based slot machines were hard to find so I shifted to slot machines based on television shows. I wanted to find one that reflected the shows of my youth—*Bonanza*, *Bewitched* and, of course, *The Beverly Hillbillies* (I've always had a thing for Elly May). Given the average age of patrons, I thought this would be a no-brainer. But none of these classic shows were to be found (Note to casinos: missed marketing opportunity!). Instead I settled down in front of a huge slot machine based on the *Big Bang Theory*, and began some serious gambling with Sheldon and the gang staring back at me the whole time. The best part about this game was that when you won, the seat shook violently for a full 15 seconds in an attempt to give you a sense of what it must have been like to live through the actual Big Bang. Sadly for me, there wasn't a whole lot of shaking going on. I lost a fair amount of money to Sheldon, Leonard, Howard, Rajesh and the others in pursuit of the vibrating chair. I should have known better than to take on a gang of scientists.

The last part of my gambling exploration was the roulette wheel. I have no idea what the strategy is for roulette, and it showed. Within minutes I went from being $120 ahead to $60 in the hole. I decided it was time to quit.

Facing retirement, I have had to accept that I, too, am getting old and will not always be the spry guy I am today. And as much as I may have poked fun at the casino's clientele, all things considered, it was not a bad place to spend some time. My friends and I had fun catching up and the damage was not that bad. I'll definitely go back with David and Gary, but next time I want to stop along the way to pick up Lady Luck. It's time for us to get reacquainted.

A quest
for knowledge

What separates humankind from the rest of the animal kingdom?

Is it our ability to make tools? Our range of emotions? Our appreciation of music? Our regular use of indoor plumbing?

This question has always fascinated me. It speaks to the very heart of our existence. And now that I have committed myself to exploring new interests, I decided it is finally time to tackle this mystery head on. So naturally, I signed up for a course in humor writing.

I'll concede that humor writing may seem like an odd choice. It isn't. For most of my life I've been convinced that what makes mankind special is our ability to laugh at ourselves, at others and at the absurdity of the world around us. This belief was turned upside down on November 13, 2016, when *The New York Times* ran an article on groundbreaking research conducted by a team of scientists in which they proved that rats can laugh and, coincidentally, that they like to be tickled. I found this to be astonishing. I can't imagine rats have much in their lives to laugh about. Ever since the Bubonic Plague in 13th century Europe, people have refused to see past the poor rats' disease-carrying reputation to embrace their warm, cuddly side. In fact, their species has become so vilified that its very name is now shorthand for those who cheat, steal, lie and double-cross. As a result, they are forced to spend their lives digging through trash cans, past the used condoms and discarded personal hygiene items, to find tiny morsels of discarded food they can take home to their families. This is not a good life. And even those lucky few who can lift themselves out of street poverty and find some nice cage to live in will likely spend their days with their brain hooked up to electrodes by some demented scientist who chases them around trying to tickle them to see if they will laugh. I can't understand how rats find humor in any of this but I'm willing to accept the scientific evidence that they do. It's given me a whole new respect for their species. It also got me wondering whether rats are the only animal other than we primates who can laugh. Can birds laugh? Or fish? What about cats? Can they laugh? After all, cats and rats are pretty closely related, separated by just one letter.

Then one day I unexpectedly put this question to the test. I walked into my kitchen and slipped on the partial remains of an ice cube that had mostly transformed into a puddle of water. My feet went out from under me. I became airborne, with my arms flailing desperately and unsuccessfully to catch myself as I fell to the floor. I came to rest flat on my back.

As I was lying there, trying to assess whether a full-body bruise was the only damage, I happened to glance over at my cat. Portia is a small, seven-pound gray feline with deep green eyes. She is the most affectionate cat I have ever known. I looked at her expecting a little sympathy. Instead I saw tears streaming down her cheeks and her jaw was hanging open. She was chortling away like an 8-year-old watching *The Three Stooges* for the first time. Occasionally she would look away, taking a few seconds to catch her breath, then glance back at me lying on the floor and the chortling would begin again. At one point, she was laughing so hard I thought she would pee her fur.

After recovering a bit, I began to wonder why Portia thought this was funny. Basically, I had done a variation of the slip-on-a-banana-peel routine, a shtick that dates back to the days of vaudeville and probably all the way back to the first caveman to slip on a pile of dinosaur poop. It is a time-tested, proven classic but admittedly not very high-brow. Yet, if my cat could find humor in a simple pratfall, I began to wonder whether she could grasp higher-level comedy like irony or satire, or perhaps even parody.

To test that, I needed to learn more about comedy.

Taking classes is a common activity among seniors. Having the time to learn more about a subject that really interests you is one of the greatest benefits of retirement. There are thousands of community colleges around the country and most give discounts to students of a mature age. With all the options, you would think finding a class about humor would be easy. It's actually quite hard. This makes no sense. Humor is a huge industry, probably generating more economic growth than all manufacturing sectors combined, possibly even more than the revenue earned from America's greatest economic resource and number one cultural asset, the Kardashians. Yet I'm willing to bet that outside of clown college, there is not a single university in the country offering a degree in "Funny." I find this funny.

I am fortunate, however. I live near one of the best nonprofit writers' centers in the country, which offered a humor-writing course that met every Saturday for three weeks. I signed up right away.

The first class found me sitting in a room with 10 other people discussing humor writing. This initially seemed very strange. I've always thought of humor as being a little like pornography—hard to describe but you know it when you see it. But the class turned out to be enlightening. We covered a lot of the basics and each did some off-the-cuff writing to share. Our instructor turned us on to "McSweeny's Internet Tendency," a web-based collection of humor pieces from various authors.

Later that night I got home and checked out the site. One piece caught my eye: "Pride and Prejudice and Trump" by Megan Quinn. I printed out a copy, settled into the Lay-Z-Boy and started to read. I was no more than a sentence or two into it when Portia jumped into my lap. She looked at me. I looked at her. She let out a big meow and pawed at the papers in my hand. She seemed interested and I thought to myself, "Why not?" I started to read the piece out loud, glancing down from time to time to see if she had any reaction. Sadly, my efforts produced nothing. No chortling. Not even a smile.

I can't say I was that surprised. Portia has never struck me as a big Jane Austen fan and she down-right hates Donald Trump (I don't think she really understood what he meant when he bragged about grabbing pussy).

A week later I was back at the writers' center. Each student was required to read a short piece they had written. I had been looking forward to this all week. It would be a great opportunity to gauge whether others saw any humor in my work. I just couldn't decide which chapter to read. My first thought was to go with an early draft of the introduction to this very chapter, but it didn't seem polished enough. So at the last minute I decided to read out loud the introduction to my chapter on golf, "Ball Challenged."

When my turn came around, I cleared my throat and started reading. About the time I got to the end of the second sentence I remembered that much of this chapter focuses on the shape of men's genitalia and includes my earnest thoughts on what you should never do with men's genitalia, topped off with some insights on the potential peculiarities of my personal set of genitalia. As I got to the part specifically referencing the shape of men's balls, I had the strong feeling that the women on either side of me were sliding back their chairs to put a little distance between us. I don't think they were alone in doing this. When I reached the part where I explained that men's balls "should never be hit, caught, dribbled, shot, thrown, bounced, served, dodged, returned, kicked or rolled," I could feel my face turning red, achieving full beet-red about the time I got to describing being 12 years old and "finally finding out the purpose behind my personal set of balls." Some of my classmates were kind enough to laugh, although it wasn't clear if this was because of the strength of the story or because of my obvious embarrassment. Either way, I was willing to accept it. I also learned an important lesson: writing lets you remain anonymous; having to read your work makes it very personal.

In the final class, we discussed various types of humor writing by different authors. On the way home, I got to thinking about all the great comics I've been exposed to during my life. It occurred to me that unless they're killed in freak banana peel accidents, they live longer than any other people on the planet. There is ample evidence to back this up. As of this writing, Jerry Lewis is well into his 90s. So is Carl Reiner. I'm not sure Mel Brooks' exact age but he claims to be more than 2,000 years old. I believe him. He has the laugh lines to prove it.

I think comedians live so long because they have trained their minds to find the absurdity in any situation. And anything that is absurd cannot be stressful. And a stress-free life is a very long life.

I too want to live a long life. Not just a run-of-the-mill long life. I want a Mel Brooks or a George Burns long life and I want my cat to live a long life as well. But even I had reached the point where I had to admit that higher levels of comedy are probably beyond Portia's ability. I was disappointed. Yet I was not ready to believe that she does not have a well-developed sense of humor. You don't live 10 years with another animal without getting to know them pretty well. I thought long, deep and hard about this and suddenly realized that laughter isn't the only way to demonstrate a sense of humor.

Portia may not laugh very often or at too many things, but one thing I am sure of is that she is the queen of the practical joke. Hardly a morning goes by when I don't find my slippers in some part of the house that I am willing to swear I did not leave them in. I would never, for example, carelessly leave my slippers lying in the middle of the living room floor, as I have often been accused of doing. Nor would I shove them so far under the bed that I need a length of rope with a grappling hook to retrieve them. Sylvia always denies any responsibility for having moved them during the night. That leaves Portia as the only possible culprit. I've confronted her over the slippers. She just smiles and walks away, as though I'm too clueless to get the joke. Then there was the night when I was sound asleep and suddenly started to dream that I was having a massive heart attack. Breathing was difficult. It felt as though there was a huge weight keeping my rib cage from expanding. I woke up to find Portia sitting on my chest with a mischievous look on her face. It was 3 in the morning and I knew she was just having a little fun with me, probably some kind of payback for buying the wrong cat food or some other injustice. One of her best practical jokes is to catch the mutant crickets that live in our basement, kill them, and carefully place their dead, partially dismembered carcasses in strategic places, like inside one of my shoes or just outside the shower door so I am sure to step on them in my bare feet. She will then sit around and wait for the dead cricket to get crushed under my full weight and for me to start yelling at her. The louder I yell, the more she seems to enjoy it. I know she finds this funny. There is no other possible explanation for why she keeps doing it.

Now that I think about it, I'm not so sure she wasn't behind the whole half-melted ice cube on the kitchen floor. And if that's the case, maybe, just maybe she already has enough humor in her life.

But enough about Portia ...

I really enjoyed taking the humor writing class. If you've found any of this book funny (and I'm guessing you did if you've gotten this far) much credit goes to the instructors and staff of the Writers Center in Bethesda, Maryland. Many thanks for all their help.

I want to be
THAT KID!

That kid is a boy about 9 or 10 years old. We're both at a bowling alley. He is two lanes to my left. I've been watching him for the last half hour, which sounds kind of creepy so let me explain before you jump to any disgusting conclusions.

That kid has the most creative bowling style I've ever seen. It's basically a combination of traditional bowling and Olympic discus throwing. Each time his turn comes around, the kid works at perfecting his style. He begins with the circular twirl of a discus thrower while holding the ball as best he can at the full extent of his arm's length. Just as he reaches the circumference of the turn he releases the ball, which crashes down the lane guided by no apparent attempt at aiming it. With every turn, the kid adds a new twist. At one point I watched, fascinated, as he executed a nearly perfect double spin, which added enough speed that the ball soared a quarter of the way down the lane before crashing to earth and heading straight for the gutter. These wonderful variations all end the same way—when he releases the ball, the sudden reduction in weight increases the kid's forward momentum. This throws off his balance and he ends up falling to the floor, lying on his back and laughing hysterically until his parents tell him he must get up so someone else can have their turn.

When I was his age, perhaps a bit younger, I used to go to the bowling alley a lot. I always had great times, but I'm not sure I ever had as much fun as he was having at that moment. But of course, I wasn't bowling. Bowling was for the adults.

My dad was a bowler. My mom was a bowler. All their friends were bowlers. In the blue-collar world of the 1960s, everyone bowled, everyone was in a league and everyone in the league had kids. Lots of kids. One evening a week, the adults would pack the children in the car and head to the lanes. Parents would bowl and kids would run wild. At any given moment, hundreds of us would be crisscrossing from one end of the building to the other for no apparent reason other than a sudden, unexplainable desire to be somewhere other than where we were, if for no other reason other than we hadn't been there yet. There was only one rule —don't leave the building. Other than that, we kids experienced a level of freedom unmatched by any of today's children. As a result, we learned early on to survive in a world of chaos. It was great.

The bowling alley had an ambiance all its own, like a well-used building long past its prime. The carpet had developed a distinctive abstract pattern from years of stains augmented every night by an unending stream of spilled sodas and globs of dropped ice cream that combined to form a never-ending work of art with we children as the artists.

There was a restaurant, if it could be called that, which served warm hot dogs grilled on metal rollers and bags of smashed chips. It was connected to a bar populated by people who looked like they had long since given up bowling, preferring instead to save what little money they had for the necessities of life, like a good stiff drink.

What I remember most was the smell, a combination of perspiration, disinfectant, burnt food and lots of cigarette smoke, so much that after every trip to the bowling alley I'd go through three days of nicotine withdrawal. I can tell you from experience that drug addiction is tough to deal with when you are 6 years old. I blame a lot of my bad behavior as a child on my tobacco cravings. My coping strategy was simple—I either had to go through detox each week or sit as close to my dad as possible while he chain-smoked through the evening TV viewing time. I usually chose the latter.

My first actual bowling experiences came much later and were usually associated with birthday parties and the occasional outing of bored teenagers who could think of nothing else to do and who annoyed their parents to the point where they would cough up some money just to get us out of the house. The highest score I ever bowled was probably 110, which I achieved sometime in my late teens. This would also be about the same age as when I last bowled. If you had asked me a year ago, I would have told you that I was almost certain to go to my grave without ever rolling another bowling ball. If that had been the case, I would not have felt at all cheated or as though I had missed out on something special. But then this retirement project came along and I realized that I had to give bowling another chance. It was one of my father's hobbies and probably the only one that got him out of the house on a regular basis. He really enjoyed it, although what I think he enjoyed most was getting together with the same people each week to socialize.

When I decided to do a chapter on bowling, my first thought was to invite my friend Jonathan and his partner Robert. I initially thought of Jonathan and Robert because of all my friends, these were the two people I would be least likely to ever run into at a bowling alley. Yet, both have an adventurous spirit and I thought they might be interested in doing something a little outside their comfort zone. Moreover, I was secretly hoping they would bring their dry wit and outstanding humor to the outing, thereby making the writing of this chapter a piece of cake, since all I would have to do was to write down everything they said. Some might consider this a form of cheating but I would like to point out that I was prepared to cover all costs associated with bowling and even throw in dinner (hot dogs grilled on metal rollers). I never got that far. Jonathan turned me down flat. Apparently, bowling had been just as big a part of his childhood as it had been in mine, with one major difference: Jonathan, as he explained it, has a pathological fear of putting on shoes that have been worn by other people. During his childhood, this had frustrated his parents to no end. They kept thinking he might enjoy bowling as much as they did. He didn't. Jonathan and Robert were out.

I knew not to call my sister Judy and her husband Mark. They gave up bowling about 10 years ago after a life-threatening bowling-related illness (no joke). The short version of the story goes like this: Mark had gone bowling with my father. He had a small cut on his finger that became infected with deadly bacteria that had found a home inside the dark, warm holes of a poorly disinfected bowling ball. The infection proved to be drug-resistant. His hand swelled up to twice its size. At one point, doctors were seriously considering amputating the middle finger of his right hand (I'm not making this up) but eventually they drained the infection and found the right drug combination to beat it back. Mark is a gutsy guy but I doubted he would be willing to risk his life again just for the sake of my book. My sister Judy and her husband were out.

I tried a few other friends, even some who lived clear across the country. All purported to be strangely busy, even before I could propose a date. Some emails went completely unanswered. Finally, after a little nudging on my part, my other sister, Karen, and her husband, John, agreed to go bowling.

Karen and John took Sylvia and me to a brand-new bowling alley in northern Virginia. I didn't even know they were still building bowling alleys but apparently they are. It was not at all like the alleys of my youth. This was obvious from the first step inside. For one thing, the restaurant looked nice, like a place you might get a decent meal and not risk food poisoning. Attached to the restaurant was a bar with a large stage for live music. The place was spotlessly clean, including the bathrooms. The only thing that hadn't really changed was the number of kids running from one end of the building to the other with no apparent purpose. I took comfort in knowing that some things stay the same.

Thirty-five dollars covered shoe rentals and three games for each of us. This seemed very reasonable. John turned out to be surprisingly good at bowling and was the only one among us who broke 100. My high game hit about 90, with only one strike and a slew of gutter balls. I felt bad about the gutter balls until I noticed the group of 13-year-old boys next to us. If the 10-year-old was the kid I wanted to be, the 13-year-olds were the kid I was. They were at that age where they had grown too fast for their bodies to keep up and, as a result, were about as coordinated as a newborn colt trying to stand for the first time. By the final frame, only one had broken 80, with the other two finishing in the 50s. Nevertheless, they seemed to be enjoying themselves despite the mother of one of them looming in the distance ready to pounce if something bad were about to befall them. Even I felt safer knowing she was there, always watching and always ready to protect us (or at least them).

The next day, Sylvia noticed the problem first. She got out of bed when the alarm went off and, in what is uncharacteristic for her, stood up and muttered,

"Holy shit." This got my attention. I watched as she started to hobble from one side of the bedroom toward the bathroom. I could tell she was in pain so I immediately leaped out of bed to offer assistance. My feet hit the floor and I stood up straight. I took my first step and nearly went down. "Holy fucking shit!" shot from my mouth. My left butt cheek felt like it had swollen to twice its size. With every step, the pain grew worse.

At first I couldn't believe that all this pain could be from bowling. I was betting that some deranged surgeon (we live near a hospital) broke into our home overnight and performed some kind of butt implant operation. The lack of any kind of incision or scar was just a testament to his (or her) skills. I was contemplating calling the police to report this crime when the phone rang.

"Does your butt hurt?" my sister asked.

"Yes."

"Does it feel like someone surgically implanted a baseball deep within your left butt?"

"Yes, only more like a basketball."

"Can you walk?"

"Barely," I said.

"I think it's from bowling."

I brought up my deranged surgeon theory but she was having none of it.

"It's the bowling alley!" She said. "We should sue! They should warn seniors! They should have made us watch a safety video or something! They should have required us to sign a waiver acknowledging the risks! They should know retirees are fragile!"

It took some doing but I calmed my sister down. I finally agreed that if the pain continued for more than a week we would join her in filing a class action lawsuit against the bowling alley, its stockholders, any relatives of the stockholders and their pets.

Fortunately for the bowling alley, stockholders and thousands of dogs and cats throughout the country, we all recovered by the third day. Not only that but we decided bowling was a lot of fun and we made plans to go back. The difference this time is that we are only going to bowl two games each instead of three. I'm also going to try that kid's technique to see if it is a little easier on the muscles. Maybe he was on to something.

Volunteering for God and country

Author's note: This chapter was written shortly after the November 2016 election. Be forewarned, I was very angry when I wrote it.

Boy, was I ever wrong.

I really believed that God wanted Hillary Clinton to become president. Looking back at the 2016 election, I saw no other possible explanation for the emergence of Donald Trump. I'll be the first to concede that Hillary was a flawed candidate. She had no defining message and seemed to believe that nuanced policy positions were an effective substitute for an articulated vision of where she wanted to take the country. Her campaign style was often flat, combining the charm of Vladimir Putin with the stiffness of Al Gore. And then there was the baggage. ALL THAT BAGGAGE! A mountain of baggage she could never climb out from under. But these faults just reinforced my belief that God was on her side. The way I saw it, virtually any person in America could have beaten her in a general election but she didn't run against anyone—she ran against Donald Trump, a former reality TV star and failed businessman who can barely string four words together into a coherent sentence and who constantly went out of his way to present himself to voters as a race-baiting misogynist. I kept coming back to the same question: How could she lose to this guy? The only way the deck could have been more stacked in Hillary's favor would have been if she had run against Bernie Madoff or Charles Manson.

Watching the early primaries and the unstoppable rise of Donald Trump, I came to the conclusion that it was all too perfect to be a coincidence. The only explanation I could come up with was that God was behind Trump's success in securing the Republican nomination as part of a larger plan to ensure Hillary Clinton would be the next president. The evidence to support this conclusion seemed substantial, especially when you consider that Trump had to defeat some serious Republicans along the way. Take Wisconsin Governor Scott Walker, for example. Here's a guy who drove his state's economy into the ground by passing massive unfunded tax cuts for the rich. He took away the rights of individuals to form unions. He defunded higher education and taxed solar energy. How could a candidate willing to carry that much of the Koch brothers' agenda not win the Republican nomination? I thought he'd be a shoe-in, but he turned out to be one of the first to drop. Then there was New Jersey Governor Chris Christie, who punished thousands of his own citizens by closing a vital bridge just because he got mad at the mayor of a town. How could he lose? All he had to do was appeal to those Republicans still longing for the petty vindictiveness of Richard Nixon. And let's not forget about "Jeb! the Inevitable." He hoped to ride his brother's legacy all the way to the Oval Office. What could possibly go wrong with that plan?

I could wade through the whole list of Republican candidates but they all shared one thing: they lost to Donald Trump. The way I saw it, only God could have made this miracle happen for Hillary.

I can't remember another election in which God seemed to play such an active role. It was hard to tell if he was directly behind the weird things that kept coming out of Trump's mouth and his Twitter account, or whether he just let Donald be Donald. Either way, I decided it didn't matter. If Hillary Clinton was good enough for God, she was good enough for me. But this realization got me wondering whether just voting was enough. If this election was so important to God, should I be doing more? After all, I suspect that God was no fan of Hitler, and Hitler still rose to power in Germany. I bet God still feels guilty about that one!

Of course, this made me wonder if God experiences guilt. We know from the Bible that he feels love for all of us, and the Old Testament says that he can become angry and vengeful. But his full range of emotions has never been clear to me. Does he feel envy? I doubt it. He's God. Who would he be envious of? What about jealousy? Does he sometimes resent all the attention his son gets? I could see that happening. Jesus is, after all, younger and better looking. But we'll never know. While I was contemplating these heavy questions, it occurred to me that maybe Hitler and World War II weren't entirely God's fault. Maybe the all-powerful creator of the universe can't do everything himself. Maybe he needs our help from time to time and, given a candidate like Hillary, he was surely going to need all the help he could get. I had to ask myself, was I prepared to face God on Judgment Day knowing that I could have done more to move his agenda on earth? The answer turned out to be a resounding no. So when the opportunity came up to volunteer for two weeks in Florida helping elect Hillary, I jumped at the chance.

I'm not much for volunteering. Yet, helping get Hillary elected was different. This was an opportunity to score major brownie points with our Lord and Savior, and that has become increasingly important to me as I get older.

Despite my cynicism about organized religion, I do believe there is a God and some kind of afterlife. I just don't hold to the traditional views of Heaven and Hell. I believe everyone goes to Heaven; we're just not all treated the same once we get there. I think the afterlife operates like an airline or hotel rewards program. The more good you do on earth, the more points you earn, and those points can be used for things like better accommodations, free trips and other heavenly perks. I know I'll never score enough points for first class or even the business section (and 72 virgins is completely out of the question), but I was hoping my two weeks volunteering to help Hillary might earn me the equivalent of an exit row aisle seat for a millennium or two.

Upon arrival in Florida, I quickly discovered that volunteering on a campaign is hard work. Very hard work. It basically involves two things: endless hours canvassing neighborhoods followed by countless hours working phone banks. Frankly, neither is a lot of fun. I was okay with it, though. Doing the Lord's work is never easy. I'm not suggesting that my sacrifice could be put in the same category as Mother Teresa's, but I am saying that I worked my butt off.

Every day began by walking mile after mile from 10 in the morning until 6 in the evening, stopping just long enough to knock on hundreds of doors of potential voters. Usually I just left campaign literature stuffed in the door, but once in a while someone would actually answer my knock. When that happened, I would follow the basic script:

"I'm campaigning for Hillary Clinton. Have you had a chance to vote yet? ... You haven't? ... Do you plan to? ... You do ... That's great ... Can Hillary count on your vote? ... She can ... That's fantastic ... Are you going to get your family and friends to vote? You are! ... Wonderful! ... Thank you so much."

I had my rap down pat. It worked great, except when I would come across a home where the person on the other side of the door spoke only Spanish. This should not have been a problem. Early in my career, I found myself going back and forth to Puerto Rico once or twice a month for nearly four years. When I started the assignment I didn't speak a word of Spanish. But through diligence and hard work, I eventually amassed an awesome vocabulary of at least 30 words. Unfortunately, all of them are related to food, drink and bodily functions. I became adept at ordering cervezas and I practiced this language skill as often as I could. I lived most days on a diet of chicken and rice because arroz con pollo was one of the few dishes I could order without help. I ate it for breakfast, lunch and dinner, and sometimes as a snack in between. I'm particularly proud of my ability to order two kinds of water—agua *con* gas and agua *sin* gas. None of those words, though, were useful in getting out the vote for Hillary. Fortunately, a young bilingual woman I met helped me out by writing down a few useful phrases:

- Donald Trump tiene la inteligencia de un mono.
- Su pelo es como las palmas de una escoba.
- Es un hombre pequeño en todo sentido.

It was much later that I learned what these phrases meant:

- Donald Trump has the intelligence of a monkey.
- His hair is like the bristles on an old broom.
- He is a small man in every way.

Not exactly uplifting arguments but I kept using them anyway. They seemed effective.

By day three, my legs hurt so badly from constant walking that I cleaned out a local pharmacy of its Icy-Hot patches. I plastered them on almost every muscle from the waist down. I looked like some kind of half-mummy, half-monster. As bad as I hurt, though, I reminded myself that suffering for God was surely going to bring me extra points—maybe not sainthood-level rewards but a lot of valuable points.

And that's what got me out of bed each morning. That's what kept me going when I didn't think I could take another step. That's what turned me into Hillary's super volunteer, happily offering to do all the three-story walk-up apartments and, when they were done, to take on all the four-story walk-ups as well. No list was too long. No turf was too scary. I gladly knocked on the doors of homes that looked barely livable. I even knocked on a few doors where the phrase "trailer trash" referred to the amount of uncollected trash piled against the trailer—so much of it in one case that the piles of garbage appeared to be the only thing keeping it from falling over.

One afternoon I knocked on a door answered by an overweight middle-age man wearing what presumably was his best answering-the-door pair of tighty-whities and nothing else. I started my opening pitch by asking the gentleman if he planned to vote. I paused to let him consider the question. This took much longer than it should have, as though the complexity of my inquiry had somehow overwhelmed his remaining brain cells.

We stood in silence until he finally looked at me and said, "You got $10?"

This response was a bit outside the norm. I had gotten used to people telling me to "get the fuck" off their property or to receiving a lecture on why Hillary was a much bigger crook than Donald. But up to that point no one had hit me up for cash. I felt I needed some clarification.

"What?" I asked.

"I need some cigarettes. You got $10?"

I thought about his request and came up with what I considered a fairly clever response, "I can't give you any money because that might be considered vote buying and that's a federal crime."

"Oh, shit, you don't have to worry about that. I'm voting for Trump," he responded.

I couldn't help but wonder why a 40-something underwear-clad guy living in a busted-up trailer was supporting Donald Trump. The only thing I could come up with was that Trump's scapegoating of Hispanics probably reinforced the guy's already existing belief that every job he had ever lost was not his fault but that of illegal immigrants sneaking into the country and clearly willing to work a lot harder than he was. Or maybe he was an eccentric trailer-park-living millionaire who desperately needed Trump's proposed tax cut to support his nicotine addiction. Either way, I really wanted to understand.

"Can I ask why you're supporting Donald Trump?"

"Because that Hillary is a cunt."

It was at this point I realized that Hillary Clinton was probably the embodiment of every unattainable woman in his life. Maybe in this context, supporting a misogynist who would lead us into a world where it is acceptable to grab women by the pussy was just the future he longed for.

I went back to my hotel and took a shower.

Several days later I encountered the canvasser's worst nightmare: dogs. I was walking on the sidewalk in front of a fenced yard when a pack of these vicious, angry animals appeared out of nowhere. There were eight of them in all. Together they formed a pretty scary group, the suburban equivalent of an Alaskan wolf pack hunting down and feasting on the old, sick and frail. I was not afraid, though. They were on the other side of the fence and besides, they were Chihuahuas—one of the smallest of all breeds. I felt safe.

The Chihuahuas followed me as I walked along the property line, yapping up a storm the whole way. None weighed more than five pounds and each, to my surprise, was small enough to fit through a tiny hole at the end of the property. Once free of their yard, they wasted no time in charging at me. I quickly realized that what they lacked in size they made up for in numbers. The only question on their mind was which would prove to be top dog by being first to draw blood. I kept an eye on the four directly in front of me while the others tried to outflank me. Before they could complete the encircling movement, I broke out into a fast, backwards run covering a good 25 yards in Olympic record-setting seconds. The Chihuahuas eventually cornered me on a neighbor's porch. I was about to give up hope and considered kicking a dog or two (which I really, really didn't want to do) when the dogs' owner appeared and demanded that they return to their yard. They complied. She then yelled at me for upsetting her precious puppies. I smiled back, knowing that risking my life in this way was certain to score me big points with the man upstairs—maybe first-class wasn't out of reach after all ... maybe even the 72 virgins?

When the walks were done for the day, the phone calling began. The concept is simple. You call someone using the same script you use on the doors. I sucked at this. I'm okay talking to people face-to-face, but put me on the phones and I become a tongue-tied idiot with less ability to put together a coherent sentence than Donald Trump. I also seemed incapable of dialing 10 digits without getting at least one of them wrong. Dialing is apparently a skill I've lost in the age of programmable smartphones.

Fortunately, my lack of skill didn't seem to matter. Phone-banking may have been effective technology 20 years ago but most people screen their calls and don't answer if they don't know the caller. Eventually, the volunteer coordinators took pity on me and kept me canvassing as much as possible.

By the eve of the election, my countless hours on the doors had given me a good view of the mood of the electorate in the part of Florida I was working.

Hispanics viewed Donald Trump with outright fear. It's not hard to see why, given his talk about building a wall; his calls for deporting millions of undocumented workers, including those whose children are U.S. citizens; his view that any judge with a Hispanic heritage is unworthy to preside over cases involving him; and his belittling of a Hispanic beauty contest winner he said was too fat. If God's intent was to scare Hispanics to the polls in record numbers, then other than selecting Lucifer himself, God could not have picked a better candidate than Donald Trump.

African-Americans were almost equally supportive of Hillary, although noticeably less enthusiastic. In all my canvassing, I only came across two African-Americans supporting Trump. For one woman, her single issue was abortion and she was convinced that Hillary would pass a law requiring all babies to be aborted. There was no point in trying to explain the truth to her. She was living in a fact-free zone. The second was a young man for whom the Second Amendment was a big issue. I pointed out that, given Donald Trump's economic program, millions of people would likely lose their jobs. This was my not-so-subtle way of insinuating that one of these jobs might be his and that his future well-being might be on the line. He wasn't buying and instead smiled knowingly then countered with, "If I got a gun, I don't need a job." I'm pretty sure he was kidding.

White women were breaking 50-50. And, as far as I could tell from my door-knocking experience, there was not a single white man in Florida voting for Hillary.

At 6 in the evening on Election Day, I knocked on my last door. Over 14 days, I had visited more than a thousand homes. All that was left was to watch the results pour in. Several volunteers and I went to a bar to catch the returns. Our mood was good, really good, until we started seeing real numbers come in. Then it got bad. Really bad. I tried to drown my sorrows in beer. That didn't work. I tried harder. I tried all night.

As I watched one state after another go for Trump, I realized how wrong I had been. Maybe God really did want Trump to win after all and his candidacy wasn't just a setup for Hillary. If that was the case, maybe I didn't score any points at all, despite my extensive volunteer efforts. Worse yet, maybe my work for Hillary had the opposite effect. Instead of increasing my chances of eternal first-class treatment, maybe my actions had condemned me to an endless afterlife in a middle seat in the last row near the bathroom. As horrible as this thought was, I couldn't believe God would ever support a candidate as crude, vulgar and dangerous as Donald Trump. Then it occurred to me that maybe God wasn't involved in this election at all. Maybe he sat it out. Maybe Trump's win simply reflected the number of Americans who were so fed up with the current system that they were willing to overlook the endless faults of a candidate with serious mental health issues because he was the only alternative to one who, in their eyes, represented the worst of the status quo.

Whatever the reason, the election is over and we have a new president. All I can say is: God help us.

Defying Death

Some people insist that the most rewarding pursuits are those that take you to the very edge—where fear and exhilaration combine to send massive amounts of adrenaline pumping through your body, producing a high unmatched by any drug.

I wouldn't know about this because I've never done it. The edge has always seemed too dangerous. As a kid, the closest I got to peering over the edge of the Grand Canyon was the edge of the parking lot. I was perfectly comfortable seeing it from a distance, and I'm okay with that. I've never felt the need to test my mettle in any activity that could result in serious injury or death. This includes but is not limited to jogging (fear of heart attack), ice skating (fear of falling through the ice and drowning) and dancing (fear of dying of embarrassment). Yet, on a conceptual level, I understand there must be something to the adrenaline rush.

A former colleague used to skydive every weekend. On Monday mornings, he would stop by my office to regale me with his experiences in words so vivid I could feel the wind against my face and share in his sensation of soaring through the clouds and floating to the earth. He eventually gave up the sport after he leaped out of a perfectly good airplane only to discover his parachute wouldn't open. Fortunately, he deployed the emergency chute and landed safely, a wet jumpsuit and slight brown spotting in the seat of his pants the only visible evidence of trauma. He shared details with me the following Monday, brown spotting and all. I missed his stories after that. I had gotten used to experiencing sky diving vicariously. His stories came as close as I needed to the real thing.

And yet, I've always had a nagging feeling that I might be missing something; that risk-taking might be the high-octane fuel needed for appreciating life. If I were serious about this book, I'd have to try at least one activity that would connect me with the natural high of an adrenaline rush. But what?

I toyed with many ideas and rejected them all. Climbing Mount Everest was out. Too cold. Sky diving was out. Fear of brown spotting. So was motorcycle riding, hang gliding, fire walking, rock climbing and visiting Chicago. All too dangerous.

But then one day on the way to visit my mom, I drove right past the solution to this dilemma. There, just off the highway, was an oddly shaped, newly constructed building with a gigantic sign hanging from the top that read, "Indoor skydiving."

Here was the perfect activity. I could go sky diving indoors, experiencing all the sensations of flying but presumably operating with a net and other safety gear.

I shot across three lanes of traffic to pull off the highway and into one of the few empty parking spots in front of the building.

I'll admit that indoor skydiving is not as dangerous as the real thing, as evidenced by the long line of 8- to 12-year-olds waiting for their turns, but it looked like a decent starting point. I sat in an observation room and watched as an enormous fan blew air with enough force to lift students and the instructor 20 to 30 feet off the ground where they soared like eagles.

This was cool!

I was going to immediately blow off the visit with my mom to join the line but realized that if I went indoor skydiving without Sylvia, she would kill me. Sylvia has no fear of flying. She has tried hang gliding, flown in an ultralight and even took flying lessons. She can stand at the edge of any cliff and enjoy it. I, on the other hand, have logged nearly 3 million air miles and still fear flying. The way I see it, every landing is no more than a controlled crash, and "water landing" is an oxymoron.

When I got home and explained to Sylvia what I had just witnessed, she was all in. We headed over the next Friday afternoon, figuring most children would be in school. We figured wrong. The place was packed with kids* and a handful of adults. More shocking was the discovery that the next available reservation was Sunday evening at 8.

Fifty-four hours later, we were once again pulling into the parking lot. Sylvia and I were teamed up with seven other flyers, most of whom were about 12 years old. We listened to the safety instructions and then suited up in our gear, which consisted of a flight suit, helmet and goggles. We were ready.

Sylvia and I took our positions at the end of the line, allowing the 12-year-olds to fly first. They showed no fear, not a care in the world. I, on the other hand, reviewed all possible calamities in my mind. How secure was the net that separated flyers from the fan below? How strong were the glass walls? How well trained were the instructors? How reliable was the equipment? I'm sure none of these questions crossed the minds of my fellow giggling flyers. Enjoy it now, I wanted to tell them, because someday you, too, will realize that you are mortal and that an unexpected death always lurks nearby. I kept my mouth shut, though, because I figured they would learn that lesson soon enough and didn't need to be creeped out by some old guy in a full-body suit with an ill-fitting helmet and goggles ranting about death and dying.

Per the instructions, each of the young flyers entered the tube through a small doorway and fell forward, being lifted into the air as the instructor helped them get into a stable position. The first flight involved hovering only five or six feet off the ground, giving each an opportunity to get used to the sensation. As they took turns, I couldn't help but notice that a wide grin would almost immediately spread across their faces. They loved it! They were flying. At the end of every flight, each flyer left the tube with a smile so big it couldn't help but make their parents feel as though it was money well spent, even if they'd raided the college fund to make it happen.

Eventually it was my turn. Like the 12-year-olds before me, I stood in the doorway and fell forward. The instructor took hold and brought me parallel to the ground as I hovered a few feet above the net. Then, without even thinking about it, I realized that I had the same big grin on my face as those 12-year-olds. I was flying. It was great. And as I hovered around in the tube, my smile kept growing wider.

I'll admit that I needed a bit more assistance than the younger flyers, but Sylvia, whose turn came next, took to it like a duck to water or, in this case, like a duck to air.

The second flight involved real soaring. Having watched others, I knew what was coming. Once the instructor stabilizes you in the tube, the fan is turned up to maximum blast. The result is that you are lifted 20 to 30 feet and then slowly drop to about five feet. This is repeated several times.

Naturally, I had some reservations about soaring. There was the potential brown spot issue combined with my own curiosity about what would happen if I threw up. Would the vomit travel to the top of the tube and stay there, or float next to me while I hovered several feet above the net? This led to a related question: How could they clean up the vomit? Which in turn led me to wonder how much vomit might already be floating around in the tube. Despite my concerns, I decided to go through with it and was glad I did. Soaring felt awesome. I'm not sure I got the full-fledged adrenaline rush you would from jumping out of a plane, but it was exhilarating, unlike anything I'd ever done.

Sadly, it was over all too quickly. Our $170 bought us a grand total of two minutes each. I suspect it's probably cheaper to jump out of a plane, but I'll have to work up to that. I figure I have time. George H.W. Bush celebrated his birthday by skydiving at age 75, then repeated the feat for his 80th, 85th and 90th birthdays. Ninety seems like a reasonable age to try it, toward the end of a long and enjoyable life, maybe sooner if I contract a terminal disease like Ebola or the Plague.

Are all kids in Virginia home schooled?

Doing nothing

Sylvia says I'm not good at doing nothing.
She's right.

I've spent most of my life doing something,
usually the kinds of things that involve planning,
scheduling and execution. It's a big part of who I am.

Some people are born to be great athletes.
Others are born with intellects so vast they can change
the world. I was born with an uncanny ability to keep
lists. This God-given talent is not all it's cracked up to
be. Personally, I'd rather have gotten the athletic or
genius genes. Then I would be rich and powerful
enough to hire someone to do planning, scheduling and
executing for me. But God never offered me a choice.
As a result, I've had to accept that I am cursed with a
knack for breaking down projects into their smallest
tasks and tracking each to its conclusion.

Early in my career, I used paper lists to track
everything—endless reams kept in two-inch binders.
These, combined with wall charts, provided a narrative

of the tasks that needed to be accomplished, along with an ongoing visual reference highlighting even the most mundane, incremental progress. Next came computerized project management applications. This was a quantum leap forward, allowing me to continuously share updated task lists with teams of staff assigned to various projects, thereby opening entirely new avenues for annoying subordinates, co-workers and supervisors alike.

I may be wrong, but I don't see a lot of planning, scheduling and executing in retirement. In fact, I suspect there may be days when I find myself with nothing to do. This concerns me. Or, to be more precise, it terrifies me. At some point in retirement, everyone must run out of things to do. It's almost inherent in the definition of retirement: when you stop putting your nose to the grindstone and can reward yourself for all your work over a lifetime by doing absolutely nothing for as long as you want.

Is this really a reward? Decades of intense work followed by years of boredom? That's exactly what I'm trying to avoid. That's half the reason I started this book. Yet, even if all the activities in this book become an important part of my retirement routine, I will no doubt occasionally find myself with blocks of time and nothing to fill them. That's not good. I get bored. I get antsy. I'm not at all sure I'll be able to adjust.

While this worries me a great deal, it scared the bejesus out of my wife. Sylvia can envision a long and horrible retirement spent with me hovering around her constantly asking what she wants to do when I really mean "*PLEASE come up with something for me to do;*

otherwise, I'll just continue to hover until I drive both of us crazy." I don't want to do that to my wife because I love her.

One of the things I love most about Sylvia is that she can go a whole day without executing a single planned activity and not feel guilty that she has somehow wasted time. Her real job involves managing multimillion-dollar projects but in her personal life she doesn't feel the need to plan and execute to feel a sense of accomplishment. She can open a book in the middle of the day and spend hours reading. She can go for a long walk without having to check first to see if there aren't some errands she can run along the way. She can spend hours without thinking about work. She can relax. She is the opposite of me.

I shared my concerns with someone close to me who does not want the forthcoming quote to be publicly attributed to her. This person suggested that I might want to practice doing nothing. Her idea was that I should take a day off and spend it acting like "a spontaneous human being rather than a programmable task monkey."

I found the monkey analogy a little hurtful. After all, there is no monkey on the planet who can keep a task list as well as I can, and I resent the insinuation that there might be. As I explained to this person, I consider myself to be the Michelangelo of list keepers, creating Gantt charts so elegant in their complexity that they are a whole new art form and destined to hang in the Museum of Modern Art or even maybe the Louvre. This person wasn't buying any of it, insisting that no one is ever going to hang a Gantt chart on their living room wall.

I eventually got over the slight. More importantly, though, I decided Sylvia (Ooops!) might have a point and that I should give her suggestion a try.

I started by putting together a list to help define what I mean by doing nothing. It's almost impossible to do nothing, unless you're a cat. We humans, even if we are doing nothing, are doing something. Watching TV is the result of a decision to do something, as is reading a book. What I mean by doing nothing is to go through a whole day with nothing planned, no activities that must be completed, no to-do list, and no scheduled tasks or events. A day of spontaneity, even if the only spontaneous decision made all day is *not* to get out of bed. And here's the most important part: I must emerge from the day of nothing without feeling the slightest bit guilty about having done nothing.

Was I up for the challenge? Could I do it? I had my doubts but was committed to giving it my best try.

My day of nothing began with enthusiasm and determination. One of my first bold actions was to make a radical departure from routine, starting with something as simple as shaving. It occurred to me, while staring at my lathered-up face in the mirror, that I not only shave every day, but I shave the same way every day. I start in the middle of the lower part of my neck, working out to the sides, moving to the cheeks and then finishing off with the chin. This routine is so ingrained in my subconscious that I don't think about shaving while I'm doing it. It's so routine, I've occasionally forgotten whether I've shaved within minutes of having done it. But not today! On my day of nothing, things would be different. I would spice up my life by doing the exact opposite of what I've been doing every day for the last 40 years. So on this morning I started with my chin, moved to the cheeks and then finished off with the neck. And the rebellion didn't stop there. My shower routine is just as rigid, always beginning with the top of my head and moving in sequence to my feet. I reversed the order for that as well. This is not as efficient as my usual routine, but who needs efficiency in retirement? I was a rebel and it felt good.

I began to wonder how far I could take the insurgency. Maybe putting on my pants both legs at a time? Shoes, then socks? Abandoning coffee with cream for cream with coffee? Eggs and bacon instead of bacon and eggs? My mind was spinning. The possibilities seemed limitless, but I reeled it back in. There simply was no way I could rush into a full-scale revolt against routine without first creating a detailed list of the pros and cons of such radical action. However, on my day of nothing, list creation was off-limits.

After the shower, I settled in for a little TV. Some argue that there is nothing good on TV, in particular, on daytime TV. I understand their point, especially as I channel-surfed past *Maury* and *Fox and Friends*, but eventually I landed on a little gem from my past—back-to-back episodes of *The Beverly Hillbillies*.

When I was 11 or 12, I loved *The Beverly Hillbillies* or, more precisely, I loved Elly May Clampett. I had a real thing for her. What's not to like? She was kind of a tomboy. She loved animals. And she had boobs, really pointy boobs. She was the total package. At that age, I had never actually seen boobs. They were mysterious and exciting and alluring and I could only imagine how awesome they must really be. It turned out that even the best of my imagination couldn't do them justice, but that's a story for another book.

Maybe it was nostalgia for my youth or a desire to rekindle my TV affair with Elly May, but I settled in to be entertained.

The most remarkable thing about *The Beverly Hillbillies* was how *unfunny* it was. Our cat Portia sat on my lap through most of the episode and even she wasn't laughing. The gist of the show was a convoluted plot about cultural adaptation that managed to be insulting to Asians while trivializing the women's liberation movement. Most of the jokes were based on how stupid the characters were. The exception was Jane Hathaway, Mr. Drysdale's secretary, the only one with any common sense. I felt sorry for her, an intelligent woman trapped in a low-paying job and surrounded by idiots, but, then again, maybe the show was an accurate reflection of how most working women felt in the 1960s.

The second most remarkable thing about the show is that it ran for eight years and was the top-rated program for two of those years (I looked this up while watching). This made me wonder whether an entire culture's sense of humor can become more sophisticated over a generation or two and, if so, how that happens. Did each generation evolve to be more intelligent or does being exposed to better comedy in our formative years make us more sophisticated consumers?

As much as I had wanted to like *The Beverly Hillbillies*, it was a disappointment. Even Elly May let me down. She, like the others, came off as being kind of clueless. On the other hand, she still had those really pointy boobs. For that reason alone, I sat through a second episode.

After more than an hour of total Lay-Z-Boy comfort, ultra 4K high-definition TV and five-channel surround sound, much of which seemed wasted on the hillbillies, I felt the need to get up and move around. I decided to go for a bike ride.

The day I got my driver's license, I parked my bike in my parent's garage, never to be seen again. At 16, driving was cool. Riding a bike was not. Then, many years ago, Sylvia persuaded me to try biking again and I love it. When I was a kid, you would almost never see an adult on a bicycle. That's not the case anymore. In the Washington, D.C., area, there are probably well over 100 miles of dedicated bike path, including the Crescent Trail just a couple blocks from our house. On any given weekend, that trail can be so packed with bikers that it has serious traffic jams complete with occasional collisions. From my house, the trail heads south to downtown D.C. or north to Bethesda, Maryland. I went north because Bethesda has a large book store.

Bookstores will eventually disappear and I will have only myself to blame, but for now it is nice to know they still exist. I spent a good hour strolling through the aisles of the Barnes and Noble picking out several interesting books I might want to read. I took pictures of the covers of each with my phone so I could later order the digital versions on my Kindle. I am obviously a hypocrite—but one with a great Kindle library.

I had lunch in Bethesda before heading home. I used to feel awkward eating alone in a restaurant. Smartphones have changed that. Now you can pretend you are checking your email as you eat. That way, people think you're a successful businessman as opposed to some pitiful old guy sitting alone in a restaurant.

A good portion of the rest of the day was spent in what should have been a short trip to the grocery store. On this particular day, I ran into one of the most common and annoying shopping experiences—someone in the 15-item-or-less line with more than 15 items. I hate when this happens. I don't know the proper social etiquette in this situation. I have learned from experience that saying something nice like, "Excuse me but this is the 15-item-or-less line" doesn't work. It is usually met with a response like "Oh, I'm just a few items over" (even though they clearly have a full cart of crap) or "I'm sorry but I'm in such a hurry" (as though the rest of us lead such impoverished lives that we have nothing better to do than stand in line at the grocery store). I have often contemplated, as I did on this particular occasion, responding with something like, "I DON'T GIVE A FUCK WHAT YOUR SORRY-ASS EXCUSE IS FOR BEING SUCH AN INCONSIDERATE LOSER BUT YOU HAVE TO GO TO THE OTHER LINE BECAUSE WHILE A SIX-PACK OF SODA MIGHT BE ONE ITEM, A CART FULL OF 24 INDIVIDUAL TUBS OF YOGURT, ALL IN VARIOUS FRUIT FLAVORS, IS NOT ONE ITEM, IT'S 24 AND EVEN IF IT WASN'T, IT WOULDN'T MATTER BECAUSE YOU STILL HAVE ANOTHER 67 ITEMS IN YOUR GOD-DAMN CART!" I held back, though, because I didn't want to create a scene. Besides, I don't think this is something that should be handled at the interpersonal level. It's a criminal justice issue.

I used to advocate for bringing back the stockade for violations of the 15-item-or-less rule. Then I decided that public flogging might be more effective. However, my views have evolved. The problem with both the stockade and flogging is that the violator remains fully capable of becoming a repeat offender. That's why I now believe in either capital punishment involving an appropriate, yet humane, method of execution or a long prison sentence guaranteed to keep the violator off the streets and out of any check-out lines for at least 20 years to life. Sylvia thinks my position is too extreme. She thinks I should consider something less drastic, like taking a page from the *Scarlet Letter* and requiring each offender to wear a giant "A" on the outside of their clothing to identify them to the entire world as an "Asshole." She has tried to persuade me that this would be sufficient punishment and would provide appropriate safeguards for the rest of society. I'm not buying it but for the sake of our marriage I've had to accept that we might not find common ground on this issue.

Speaking of Sylvia, I was thrilled when she finally got home. More than that, I felt overwhelmed by the opportunity to interact with another human being. And that, I realized, was the first big problem with my day of doing nothing. It was devoid of other people. I had only myself and my cat to entertain me. The closest interaction I'd had all day with another human was the check-out clerk at the grocery store and the waitress at the restaurant. That might be enough human contact for a day or two, but three or four days like this would be brutal. If I am going to thrive in retirement, I need to find a larger circle of friends.

The second problem was the amount of TV viewing. I probably watched more than three hours of TV, and that does not include what I watched that evening with Sylvia. I love TV. It's entertaining and requires very little effort. The actors, producers, writers and directors do all the work for us, thereby letting us close down whole sections of our brains. I'm not sure that's a good thing. It could lead to mental atrophy in retirement. My brain is already headed in that direction. It doesn't need any additional help.

I had expected to feel some guilt about wasting an entire day and accomplishing nothing meaningful, but strangely, I didn't feel any at all. Then it occurred to me that maybe the reason I wasn't feeling guilty was because I hadn't really done nothing. What I'd actually done was schedule an entire day of doing nothing so I could write a chapter about it. The whole premise of my experiment was flawed.

And yet, I learned a lot from the experience. Doing nothing is hard and I'm not good at it. I'll concede that this was my first real try and that, over time, I may get better. But it won't be easy. If I'm going to have a successful retirement, I'll need to really work at this. And if I'm going to have any chance at all, I'll need a plan, complete with a well-developed task list, schedule, benchmarks, milestones and wall charts to track progress.

Lessons learned

Work has been a big part of my life for a very long time. My first job, at 16, was clean-up boy at a neighborhood Dunkin Donuts. My duties included throwing out stale donuts every evening, then climbing into the dumpster and jumping up and down on them to make room for the next day's batch of expired merchandise. At the end of each shift, I would emerge from the bin with all kinds of jellies, creams, chocolate and other gooey fillings caked to my pants from my soles to my waist, along with glazes, powdered sugar and multicolored jimmies. Every yellowjacket within 20 miles would join me on my nightly donut-smashing odyssey, with most harassing me all the way home. Yellowjackets, I learned, are surprisingly fast and can easily outpace a fleeing teenager.

Fortunately, the job didn't last. I was fired after two weeks. Apparently, the owner was not impressed with my donut-smashing abilities.

I moved on to a job at a department store where I, along with a dozen other kids my age, worked in the stockroom taking merchandise off trucks, putting price stickers on each item and sending them out to the floor to be sold. It was mind-numbing, tediously boring work made just bearable by the large amounts of pot we would smoke before our shifts and on each break.

Yet, these two jobs, more than any others, changed my life. I came away from these early experiences having reached one important conclusion: I was definitely going to college. I'm not saying that I was particularly smart. My high school grades would never support that claim, but I was just smart enough to know that a college degree would open opportunities for more engaging work. The way I figured it, if I had to spend 40 hours a week doing something, I wanted it to be fun or at least challenging. Donut smashing didn't cut it, nor did affixing price labels onto truckloads of light bulbs, a task that went on for weeks in preparation for the store's annual extravaganza, the "We Light Up Your Life" sale. Occasionally, for fun, I would put stickers on a few random bulbs with an unusually high price point, say, $99,999.99. I like to think that, in my own way, I was helping the store reach its quarterly profit goals.

All good things come to an end. Eventually I was off to college with a personal pledge to do just enough to get by. With a lot of determination on my part, I succeeded in achieving this goal despite the expectation of some professors that I would actually study.

After graduation, I went out into the work world where, with a bit of luck and a whole lot of actual hard work, I eventually landed a great job that was uniquely aligned with my skill set and that provided the opportunity to do a lot of good while being reasonably well paid. I was lucky. Very, very lucky. Most people don't get the level of satisfaction at work that I did. Mine was the kind of job where it was easy to get excited by just about every assignment I was given. Most were challenging, interesting and fun.

Then they stopped being that way. There were a lot of reasons I don't need to go into, but a big part of it was that after more than 46 years of working, with more than half of that being with the same employer, I felt I had accomplished all I could and that it might be time for a big life change. I couldn't picture myself being one of those people who die at their desk. On the other hand, I was haunted by the question of what to do in place of work. For all my complaints, work does provide a sense of purpose and a community of colleagues and friends. It also fills a lot of time.

This book was written over the course of a year while I was still working. I started it because I didn't want to fly blind into retirement. I wanted to experience it before making a commitment. So, I made a pledge to cut back on the 50+ hour work weeks, adopt a more normal work schedule and use the extra time to explore new adventures and to reconnect with the interests of my youth. And I did just that. I stopped answering most email in the evenings. I stopped working weekends unless really necessary. I started using the newly freed-up time to have fun.

What did I learn from this journey?

A lot. In fact, I believe I've discovered three Cs for a successful retirement: Community, Creativity and Contribution.

Community: What was most fun about the activities in this book was doing them with other people. Whether it was fishing with an old friend, taking classes with my wife, gambling with former co-workers or go-cart racing with my sister and her husband, I had a group of people to share the experience with. What I also discovered, though, was that I need a bigger circle of friends. I don't think this is going to be as easy as it sounds. Work has a way of throwing people together. Even introverts like myself are forced to interact with other people. Connecting with new people in retirement is going to be hard. With any luck, I'll have time to work on this.

Creativity: Woodworking and writing are terrific creative outlets and I look forward to having more time for both. I particularly enjoyed rediscovering how much I like writing. This book forced me to get out and try new things I would not have if it weren't part of a project. In a way, the book became a second job—only one that was fun and had no deadlines. The downside of creative pursuits is that they tend to be solo activities.

Contribution: I plan to get more involved in political activities. I enjoyed my volunteer work on behalf of Hillary Clinton's campaign. It was great to spend time with like-minded activists. We didn't win, but I have the feeling there are going to be opportunities over the next few years to become more politically engaged. That is, of course, unless my progressive views end up getting me sent to some future Trump re-education camp. If that does happen, I just hope they allow conjugal visits.

I've been asked which activity I enjoyed most. Except for yoga, I've enjoyed every stop in this adventure. I plan to do more kayaking, fishing and cooking, and am hoping to start some new adventures. I want to try pottery and jewelry making. I also plan to travel more.

That leaves one last question: When will I retire? While retirement is far less frightening than it was when I started this book, it is still hard to pull the trigger. My plan now is to retire in six to 12 months. That is, of course, unless I get a publisher and this book ends up on *The New York Times* best sellers list. Then maybe six to 12 weeks. You can help make this happen by recommending this book to your family and friends.

For information on other books by Lawrence Doyle
visit LGDoyle.com

Made in the USA
Coppell, TX
20 May 2020

25993400R00118